LIVING
IN THE LIGHT
OF DEATH:
Existential Philosophy
in the Eastern Tradition,
Zen, Samurai & Haiku

by
Frank Scalambrino

Castalia, OH: Magister Ludi Press
MMXVII

Castalia, OH: Magister Ludi Press; first printing 2017.

Scalambrino, Frank

Includes bibliographic references.

ISBN-10: 0998870404

ISBN-13: 978-0-9988704-0-3

1. Zen (Philosophy) 2. Samurai (Philosophy)

3. Haiku (Poetry)

10 9 8 7 6 5 4

Front Cover Images: Public Domain Images: Yoshitoshi (1886), "100 Aspects of the Moon," Nos. 16, 27, and 62.

Back Cover Background Image: Public Domain: Yoshitoshi (1883), "Cherry Tree on the Sumida River."

Back Cover Images: Public Domain Images: Yoshitoshi (1886), "100 Aspects of the Moon," Nos. 3, 24, 25, 93, and 100.

Back Cover Bottom Left Image: (cc) "Lord of Death" in Vajrayāna Buddhism. Redtigerxyz at English Wikipedia: (https://commons.wikimedia.org/wiki/File:Yamantaka_Vajrabhairav.jpg), Yamantaka Vajrabhairav, https://creativecommons.org/licenses/by-sa/3.0/legalcode.

Cover design by Frank Scalambrino.

In compassion, for the liberation of all sentient beings.

(Read this out loud)
I send my heart along with the sound of this voice.
May the hearer awaken from forgetfulness and transcend
all anxiety and sorrow.

"There is surely nothing other than the single purpose of the present moment... If one fully understands the present moment, there will be nothing else to do, and nothing else to pursue."   ~ T. Yamamoto (2011: 76).

"To be shifted from the world of life into the world of death is, for the flower, a kind of transcendence. The flower made to stand upon death has been cut off from the constructs of time that occur in life, and it is just as though it stands in the timeless present... shifted to this transcendent moment and fixed there. It becomes a temporary manifestation of eternity that has emerged in time."
                                        ~ K. Nishitani (1995: 25).

"Will you try to find some better expression for death? When you find it, you will have quite a new interpretation of your life."   ~ Shunryu Suzuki (2011: 84).

"As long as you keep death in mind at all times, you will ... avoid myriad evils and calamities... What is more, your character will improve and your virtue will grow... When you always keep death in mind, when you speak and when you reply to what others say, you understand the weight and significance of every word..."
                                        ~ T. Shigesuke (1999: 3).

"The Five Remembrances:
1) I am of the nature to grow old; there is no way to escape growing old.
2) I am of the nature to have ill health; there is no way to escape having ill health.
3) I am of the nature to die; there is no way to escape death.
4) All that is dear to me and everyone I love are of the nature to change. There is no way to escape being separated from them.
(Alternative: "Everything that I cherish and value today I shall have to be separated from in the future.")
5) I inherit the results of my actions of body, speech, and mind. My actions are my continuation.
(Alternative: "My only true inheritance is the consequences of my actions of body, speech, and mind. My actions are the ground on which I stand.")
~ Thich Nhat Hanh (2009: 175).

"Everyone says that no masters of the arts will appear as the world comes to an end. This is something that I cannot claim to understand. Plants such as peonies, azaleas and camellias will be able to produce beautiful flowers, end of the world or not. If men would give some thought to this fact, they would understand."
~ T. Yamamoto (2011: 122).

"The drowning person is in the water,
The rescuer is also in the water.
Their being in the water is the same,
But their reason for being in the water is different."
~ Zen Sand (Hori, 2003: 618).

Table of Contents

Acknowledgements

My friends shall understand that in the midst of such transitoriness and impermanence there is no reason for us to list names here.

I received no outside funding or sabbatical with which to write this book.

Preface

Despite whatever we may accumulate, we all must cope with the conditions of existence. For as long as we have existed, we have been coping with these conditions. Looking to "ancient wisdom schools," it may be possible to discover insights which have not been preserved by the "main stream" of our present culture. This book seeks to share a moment of lucidity in the search regarding the great mystery of the human condition known as "Death."

I first encountered Zen at the age of 18 at Kenyon College. Two monks, who identified as "Zen Buddhists," visited campus to provide free lessons on "how to meditate." I am no longer certain what I expected or what precisely motivated me to participate in the lessons. I find it amusing to think, now, how difficult it was to find anyone to attend the event with me. In attendance at the event were two monks, myself, and the one friend I was able to find who was willing to participate.

To my mind at the time, all I did that evening was sit down on a cushion in front of the monks and follow their instructions. These instructions amounted to taking a certain posture and counting my breaths in cycles of five. However, my experience that evening was so profound that – I recognize in hindsight – it changed me forever.

Throughout the years I have participated in meditation groups and taught meditation and mindfulness techniques to future clinical psychologists, (including hosting "Mindfulness Mondays" at The Chicago School of Professional Psychology in downtown Chicago, Illinois), and to undergraduate philosophy and psychology majors; I now teach meditation and aspects of Zen Buddhist philosophy in introduction to existential philosophy and introduction to ethics courses. In fact, providing a resource for my students was the primary motivating factor which caused this book to exist.

The first chapter of this book speaks directly to the insights gained from what may be called the practice of "living in the light of death." It is my hope that the communication of these insights is concise enough to be accessible at an introductory-level, despite any depth that may be attributed to Zen Buddhist and Existential insights into the "metaphysics of time." The second chapter provides an introduction to the history and theory of Zen with special focus on the notions of "Karma," "Enlightenment," and "Attachment." The third chapter provides an introduction to the practice of Zen, with special focus on mindfulness and Zen.

The remainder of the book examines the existential import of Zen regarding the way of the samurai and the construction of haiku poetry, especially in relation to the Zen tradition of kōan study involving "capping phrases." In examining the "history of Japanese existential philosophy" one learns to see the spirit of Zen woven through the violence of the samurai and the beauty of masterful haiku poems alike. Of course, there is an ethics involved here; however, perhaps even more striking is the consistent presence of the Japanese aesthetic in relation to this common thread of Zen. In this way, the spirit of Zen may also be found in devotion to one's work, to one's art, and to one's death.

Just as Zen Buddhists take "impermanence" to be one of the three characteristics of reality, so too "impermanence" is often the word used to depict "the Japanese aesthetic," i.e. Zen as the "flowering of one's nature." It is as if the blossoms of the cherry tree – being beautiful and fragrant, yet dying shortly after they bloom – increase their beauty and power by embracing impermanence, not by attempting to deny it. In this way, it is as if *the truth* of the existence of the cherry blossom is revealed "in the light of death." As such, insofar as the cherry blossom *truly* is what it is, then it lives in the light of death.

North Canton, Ohio.
Winter, 2017.

I.
Living in the Light of Death

"Our life is transient and fragile, always threatened by death.
However, the strength of life itself lies in its transience.
All the brilliance and strength is found where human beings
can live only once and each one of our steps carries us to death
as the thorough negation of ourselves."
~Takeuchi, (2011: 177).

§1 *This Floating World: The World-ing Process*

In this section we will discuss what may be referred to as the "Buddhist idea of non-substantiality." This idea is quite foreign to Western philosophy, insofar as the Western Tradition is founded on, not only the idea of substantiality but also, the quest to discover substance. After briefly examining the idea of substance, then, we will discuss the value of this Buddhist idea in terms of the clarity it provides regarding the truth of reality and the truth of our own be-ing.

The idea of "substance" suggests that there is some-*thing* that "stands under" or "behind" the human understanding of a situation. Though the idea of non-substantiality also refers to the individual objects of experience, for our purpose here we will only consider situational experiences. Simply put, a momentary experience of a situation is composed of multiple parts. In order for us to comprehend a situation we must compose various parts of the moment's information under an idea. Because we use these ideas to comprehend situational-experiences, we will call these "comprehensive-ideas." The problem, then, is that though comprehensive-ideas function conveniently for us to comprehend our sensory experiences, it is not necessarily true that these ideas refer to anything substantial in reality.

For our purpose we will understand this in two ways. First, the relation between comprehensive-ideas and non-substantiality may be understood by considering the meaning of "impermanence." Second, that to which a comprehensive-idea is supposed to refer may be understood as non-substantial by cultivating a *practice* of "be-ing awake." This second way is "living in the light of death." We will understand this at a deeper level later; suffice to say at this point, repeatedly relating to these comprehensive-ideas as though either they no longer refer to something that once existed or they refer to something non-substantial, i.e. the ideas are illusory-by-nature, may be compared to be-ing in a continual process of dying.

The two comprehensive-ideas on which we will focus in this book are: "the world" and "the self." Of course, this also includes other selves. Thus, if the ideas of "the world" and "the self" do not refer to substantial reality, then relating to these ideas as if they are substantial, fetters us to suffering and obscures our experiences with illusions. Yet, at the same time, living life repeatedly awake to the non-substantiality of these ideas – especially at first for Westerners – is like repeatedly experiencing the death of the world, the death of others, and the death of yourself. Superficially this may be like saying every moment is unique like a snowflake and, therefore, cannot be duplicated – meaning the end of the moment is the end of the never-to-be-duplicated snowflake; however, at a deeper level, this is the loss of everything and everyone you love.

To be clear, here is a summary of what has already been said. (1) Comprehensive-ideas, which are pragmatic and functionally useful, have no substantial reality. (2) To live in relation to such ideas as if they have substantial reality is to experience suffering and a mind obscured by illusions. (3) To live in relation to such ideas as if they are non-substantial is to witness human experience as if it were happening within a continual process of dying. (4) The practice of remaining awake, i.e. not believing in the substantiality of the comprehensive-ideas, is "living in the light of death," aka "the practice of dying." (5) The tendency to "hypostasize," i.e. take the comprehensive-idea of "the world" as substantial, is called the "world-ing process."

Taking the above five summary thoughts as our point of departure, we should now be able to see that we have control over the tendency to hypostasize "the world." In other words, insofar as it is true that hypostasizing "the world" breeds illusion and suffering, then we have the power to be saved from the illusions and sufferings associated with hypostasizing "the world." How would we be saved from such suffering and illusion? Stop believing in the substantiality of "the world." Why is this difficult to accomplish? Because of our *desire* for "the world" to be substantial. In fact, the same goes for the other comprehensive-ideas, including the idea of your "self."

We will now begin a discussion of our role in the world-ing process and its relation to death. Though the next two comments will not become fully clear until the end of the next chapter, here we can say: One, Buddhism's mixture with Japan's indigenous understanding of spirituality, i.e. Shintōism, resulted in Zen Buddhism's awareness of "living in the light of death." Two, several of the aspects of Buddhism familiar to Westerners relate directly to our role in the world-ing process, we will briefly discuss "attachment and clinging," "the five skandhas," and "the four noble truths" here.

The following two Japanese sources point to the above insights concretely and abstractly, respectively.

The most difficult problem of all for man to face is the oncoming of death. The problem as to how to face death has developed in Japan as a peculiar pattern of culture. It makes the Japanese feel that they must meet death squarely, rather than avoid it. The cultural tradition encourages them to be prepared to accept death with courage and with tranquility. So how one faces death has come to be regarded as an important feature of life. Death is not a mere end of life for the Japanese. It has been given a positive place in life. In that sense, it may well be said that for the Japanese *death is within life* [emphasis added]. (Hideo, 1967: 119).

3

Rather than provide the Buddhist account of why "oncoming of death" may be "the most difficult problem of all," as it was called in the above quote, consider the following from a philosophical discussion of the Japanese art of flower arranging.

> From the perspective of their fundamental nature, all things in the world are rootless blades of grass. Such grass, however, having put roots down into the ground, itself hides its fundamental rootlessness. Through having been cut from their roots, they are, for the first time, made to thoroughly manifest their fundamental nature – their rootlessness. To be shifted from the world of life into the world of death is, for the flower, a kind of transcendence. The flower made to stand upon death has been cut off from the constructs of time that occur in life, and it is just as though it stands in the timeless present... (Nishitani, 1995: 25).

Thus, the notion of "death within life" from the first block quote coincides with being "cut off from the constructs of time" in the second block quote, i.e. what the Japanese philosopher Nishitani – invoking the perennial existential vocabulary – refers to as "the timeless present."

In this way, "living in the light of death" may also be understood as living in the "timeless present," and Buddhism may be understood as so many approaches to illuminating the path of living in the "timeless present," i.e. "living in the light of death." Moreover, there are direct ethical consequences,

> When you assume that your stay in this world will last, various wishes occur to you, and you become very *desirous*. You want what others have, and cling to your own possessions, developing a mercantile mentality.
>
> When you always keep death in mind, covetousness naturally weakens, and to that degree a grabby, greedy attitude logically does not occur. That is why I say your character improves. (Shigesuke, 1999: 5).

4

Notice, as the above quote suggests, hypostasizing the comprehensive-ideas of "the world" and "the self" fuels desire. This is often characterized in terms of "attachment" and "clinging" to materiality, as if the things of "the world" could permanently remain in our possession and as if we will never die. Thus, these are two ways we may gain control over the world-ing process, i.e. by keeping in mind that things in "the world" are impermanent and that we will die. Yet, beyond our relation to materiality, a hypostasis of "the self" and the habit-establishment of "points of view" reciprocally-reinforce each other. This is why the "world-ing process" may be easier to see than the "self-ing process."

The following quote from the Zen master Dōgen not only speaks against hypostasizing "the world," i.e. against worldliness, but also against being desirous of affectations rooted in the comprehensive-idea of "the self."

> The mistake that has arisen among students here is that they consider the respect of others and the forthcoming of property and riches to be the manifestations of virtue; and other people also know that and think so too. Knowing in your heart that this is the affectation of the demons of temptation, you should be most deliberate. In the Teachings this is called the doing of demons. I have never heard, among the examples of the three countries [India, China, and Japan], that one should regard material wealth and the reverence of the ignorant as virtues of the Way. (Dōgen, 2007; quoted in Cleary, 2008: 5).

The Western contemporary way of articulating this rootedness in the supposed-substantiality of self would be in terms of "ego." Buddhists have a way of discussing how the "ego" sprouts, i.e. arises, from rootedness in such hypostasizing of "the self."

For example, according to *The Tibetan Book of Living and Dying*,

> Once we have a physical body, we also have what are known as the five skandhas – the aggregates that compose our whole mental and

physical existence. They are the constituents of
our experience, the support for the grasping
ego, and also the basis for the suffering of
samsara. (Rinpoche, 2009: 254).

Because "Skandha" is a Sanskrit word meaning
"aggregate" or "heap" or "accumulation," the five skandhas
are also known as the Five Aggregates. Importantly, on the
one hand, "All the teachings presented by the Buddha in
the sutras, whether they deal with the Basis for the Path,
the Path itself, or the Fruit of the Path, can be subsumed
under the topic of the five skandhas." (Rinpoche, 1986:
139). On the other hand, "The study of the five skandhas
is important because it directly relates to our habitual
tendency to cling to a self." (Ibid.)

Associated with the senses, the five skandhas are:
(1) Forms or Material Forms, (2) Sensations or Feelings,
(3) Recognition, (4) Volitional Formations or Karmic
Fabrications, and (5) Consciousness. (1) "Material Forms"
may be divided in terms of "causes" and their "effects." The
four kinds of Material Forms are referred to as "Earth,
Water, Fire, and Air," referring "to all the many things
perceivable by the eye and other sense organs." (Rinpoche,
2009: 140). (2) There are five types of Sensations or
Feelings, "three basic types of bodily sensation:
pleasurable, painful, and neutral. Mental sensations can
be pleasurable or painful. The neutral mental sensation, or
the feeling of equanimity [tranquility, a kind of perfection],
is not different from the neutral bodily sensation." (Ibid:
149). (3) The Third Aggregate is Recognition. "This is
grasping at characteristics, which is synonymous with
clinging to samsara [the phenomenal "world"] as being real
and permanent." (Ibid: 150). We will discuss "samsara" in
the next chapter.

Whereas the Second Aggregate "Sensation" is direct,
"Recognition" refers to the "grasping at the object" to which
sensation is supposed to be directly related. This grasping
may be divided into perceptual and conceptual grasping.
When we grasp sense-derived attributes of the object it is
perceptual, and when we recognize the object in terms of
its conceptual differences or understanding its symbolic
references, then the grasping is conceptual. The (4) Fourth

6

Aggregate is known as "Volitional Formations" or "Accumulated Volitions Shaping Aggregates" or "Karmic Fabrications" because it involves the particularized way each of us "form" together or comprehend the other Aggregates, i.e. "what kind of activity is performed in the mind" (Rinpoche, 2009: 151). In other words, when our habitual (karmic) ways of interpreting (fabrications) and responding (acting) are triggered, then the Fourth Aggregate is involved.

Given space constraints here, all of the aspects of the Aggregates cannot be fully explicated; for those interested in such an explication, see Kalu Rinpoche's *The Dharma: That Illuminates All Beings Impartially Like the Light of the Sun and the Moon*. For our purpose, though, we should consider that there are "five *omnipresent* mental occurrences" associated with the Fourth Aggregate (Ibid). It is important to notice that these mental occurrences include the previous two mental Aggregates. On the one hand, this is why Aggregates two through four are sometimes referred to as the "mental factors." On the other hand, this is why the Fourth Aggregate is referred to as "Accumulated Volitions Shaping Aggregates." The "five *omnipresent* mental occurrences" are (a) Intention, (b) Concentration, (c) Contact, (d) Feeling (Aggregate 2), and (e) Recognition (Aggregate 3).

In the sutra known as *The Great Full-Moon Night Discourse (Mahā-Punnama Sutta)*, referring to the third of the five omnipresent mental occurrences, Buddha is quoted as explaining the "dependent origination" of reality, noting that "Contact" with the Aggregate or Accumulation associated with the "four great elements" of earth, water, fire, and wind (or air), constitutes "the connection of the mind to its object" (Ibid). In regard then to the last Aggregate (5) Consciousness, it is said to be dispersed in relation throughout the five omnipresent mental occurrences. Further, consciousness is associated with the five senses and, sixthly, with "mind consciousness," conceiving "the mind as a sense faculty because it can recall past events and perceive various mental objects." (Ibid: 171). Thus, "Through all six types of consciousness, one can know distinctly the nature and characteristics of

7

phenomena," that is to say, with "the support of the sense faculty, the corresponding intelligence arises." (Ibid).

What is important for our purpose is the quality of "Contact" with phenomena being aggregated into the object of experience. When the Contact is characterized by "clinging," for example, due to craving or desire, then the Volitional Formation (Aggregate 4) is subject to clinging. In this way, on the one hand, the phenomena of experience are conceived as objects of experience, and, on the other hand, the phenomena of experience are aggregated as objects of desire. Clinging to the aggregates involves the comprehensive-ideas of "the world" and "the self." For example, clinging to the Accumulated phenomena in terms of appropriation is rooted in the comprehensive-idea of "the world" in that there follows an attempt to possess, or hold as property, the Accumulated phenomena comprehended as objects of desire in "the world." Likewise, the comprehensive-idea of "the self" is involved in clinging to the Accumulations in terms of identification. This would be to relate to the skandhas in order to identify your self, e.g. "I" am this body or "I" am the subject of these desires or "the self" to whom these desires belong (cf. Lodrö, 1992: 190; cf. Ñāṇananda, 1997: 84). Of course, when clinging involves the hypostasized comprehensive-ideas such as "the world" and "the self," the individual may be said to be involved in illusion and suffering due to ignorance and desire.

Lastly, there are three characteristics Buddhists associate with all of the Aggregates, i.e. "impermanence" (*anicca*), "suffering" or "unsatisfactoriness" (*dukkha*), and "non-substantiality" (*anattā*). Insight and wisdom, then, regarding these characteristics lead to liberation from the illusion and suffering stemming from ignorance and desire involving the hypostasized comprehensive-ideas of "the world" and "the self." Thus, for example, we find the Four Noble Truths articulated in terms of "suffering" or "unsatisfactoriness" (*dukkha*). The first truth is the truth of suffering; second, the truth of the arising of suffering; third, the truth of the cessation of suffering; fourth, the truth of the path leading to the cessation of suffering. This path is referred to as the Noble Eightfold Path. Whereas the first two Noble Truths refer to "Samsara," the last two refer to "Nirvana."

As we will discuss in the next chapter, there is a clear association between realizing the non-substantiality of "the world" and "the self" and the cessation of suffering discussed regarding "Nirvana" (cf. Scalambrino, 2014). This theme, then, of liberation from the illusion and suffering associated with "the world" and "the self" is epitomized by the practice of "living in the light of death." And, as we will see, this practice extends across Zen Buddhist monks, the samurai, and Japanese haiku poets. As the famous samurai manual, the *Hagakure*, suggests, we should

> see the world as a dream. When you have something like a nightmare, you will wake up and tell yourself that it was only a dream. It is said that the world we live in is not a bit different from this. (Yamamoto, 2011: 86).

Moreover, to take refuge, then, from the suffering of, for example, "the world," points to the Three Jewels of Buddhism, i.e. the Buddha, the Dharma, and the Sangha. At the same time, in order to approach illuminating the non-substantiality to which the comprehensive-idea of "the self" is supposed to refer, the following three sections are framed in terms of temporality, i.e. the time in which we would find our-"selves."

§2 *Futural Be-ing*

There are two guiding questions for this section. First, is there a way to relate to your "futural be-ing," i.e. your be-ing in the future, such that a kind of communication takes place which transcends time? Notice, this question need not assume the substantiality of "the self." In other words, is there a kind of communication that takes place across time as if the two moments which are in communication are thereby "outside" of the temporal-flow, i.e. "outside" the temporal flow which otherwise suggests they are "distant" from each other? Second, is there a way to "merge" with your future be-ing through (a kind of non-physical) "death," i.e. "living in the light of death"?

In regard to the first question, the word "your" in the phrase "your be-ing in the future" may be perplexing. For example, you may wonder how does the word "your" have meaning in the light of non-substantiality? For our purpose we may think of that to which "your" is supposed to refer simply in terms of the continuation of that which we call "your consciousness" or the tendencies of the First and Fourth Aggregates constituting "your karma." In the second question the word "merge" may be perplexing, since, on the one hand, there is no substantial self in either moment for them to be "merging." On the other hand, if the be-ing in both of these moments is "your" be-ing, then wouldn't it be the case that they are already "merged"?

For our purpose, then, we may understand "merge" in two ways. First, recognizing that the be-ing in both moments is already "your" be-ing, we may think of "merge" in terms of "reveal" or "unconceal." In this way, it is as if the illusory nature of the passage of time is transcended by the awareness of be-ing "outside" time's passing, i.e. the Volitional Form's relation to the Accumulations reveals the passage of time as illusory for "your" be-ing. Second, in order for us to understand the "merging" here in terms of non-substantiality, we need to recognize the relation both moments have to the form of this revelation.

We can now answer the guiding questions. Notice that the content of your thinking in a present moment can be the content of your memory in a future moment. Further, notice how this can be seen in either "direction." That is, we can choose to sustain a thought about something now (or study something now), so that our memories in the future will be filled with our chosen images and thoughts. In the other "direction" (i.e. "from the future"), when we realize the *form* of this truth *now*, it is the same form which will be realized in the future. In other words, in a future now the realization of this truth – that the content of experience now will be a memory in the future – participates in the same timeless form. The form transcends the passage of time, and therefore it is in terms of the form that the be-ing of this moment both "merges" and "communicates" with the future be-ing. Thus, we are looking for a form.

This form may be called "living in the light of death." Why? Because when we "fall out of" this form, what we need to *remember* (to re-turn into the awareness of the form) is the non-substantiality of "the world" and "the self."

Thus, we may enumerate the following aspects associated with "living in the light of death," all of which relate to an awareness of impermanence and non-substantiality associated with the "futural be-ing." Don't let the philosophical terminology intimidate you, we will discuss each term. There is an "ontological," "soteriological," "teleological," and "eschatological" aspect to "living in the light of death." The ontological aspect, i.e. the aspect that pertains to "your" be-ing, is the one we emphasized above; it is as if we recognize our present be-ing extends throughout and transcends the passage of time. Some Buddhists push this further and suggest that the form of thinking is the *form* of enlightenment discovered by the Buddha, and, therefore, when we discover enlightenment, we discover "the mind of Buddha." At the same time, some Zen Buddhists suggest the eternal nature of the form may be differentiated from any self which may be associated with its discovery.

The soteriological aspect, i.e. the aspect that pertains to salvation, brings the Four Noble Truths into the conversation. That is to say, by participating in the form of Zen or "living in the light of death," the properly form-ed impermanence and non-substantiality lead to the cessation of the third characteristic of human existential reality, i.e. suffering. The teleological aspect, i.e. the aspect that pertains to the purpose and meaning of life, emphasizes the potential inherent in human existence to actualize or realize enlightenment. In other words, it is as if the power to become enlightened naturally belongs to every human, since the "structure" of the human existential condition is universal for the human species.

Finally, the eschatological aspect pertains to the ending of existence. This may be understood in three ways. First, recalling the Five Remembrances, the vital power of this body will end. Second, the clinging which constitutes the Accumulations, aka the Aggregates or skandhas, can end; however, according to Buddhism, the clinging will not necessarily end with the death of the body. These two endings can, but do not necessarily, coincide. Third, the futural be-ing accomplishes its death by realizing impermanence and non-substantiality – that is, by properly in-forming the stream of accumulating, which we may call "its past." In the moment that the futural be-ing accomplishes this, its past be-ing is liberated by the in-formation. Because, *prior to the liberation,* the futural be-ing's past be-ing was experiencing be-ing in terms of a present moment, clinging, in the temporal-flow of Accumulations, the present be-ing receives the in-formation "in the light of death," i.e. as a kind of death.

Put more simply – by not sustaining the following in relation to an awareness of non-substantiality – (and notice how this connects with our discussion from the beginning of this section), when you begin to think *now* about your own death, i.e. your own impermanence, it is a memory for you in the future. As you sustain this "loop with yourself," it is as if you are "living in the light of your own death." Finally, two comments about this "loop." One, this "loop" provides an awareness of a "you" which transcends time, i.e. which transcends the temporal distance between the present you and the future you. Two, this "loop" is the *form,* i.e. it is the Volitional Form Recognizing the truth in regard to Contact with "the world" in light of impermanence and non-substantiality; "living in the light of death."

Finally, for ease of communication, in terms of these "three yous," initially it seems as if the looping of your (1) present and (2) future selves manifests a (3) transcendent-self "outside" of time. However, from a higher perspective, realize that the transcendent-self would be the origin-al self and the "other selves" were always already illusions manifested through clinging to the Accumulations. Of course, be-ing mindful of non-substantiality, there is no original "self." That "dimension" to which "original self" refers in this paragraph is the ultimate condition for be-ing awake, which is revealed by the proper Volitional *form.*

To sum in different words, the thoughts of the (1) present you about your death in-form the memories for you to have when you (2) die in the future, (3) you thereby "die" to the passage of time, i.e. by realizing your impermanence

12

(3) you wake in a *form* of impermanence (*anicca*) and realize non-substantiality (*anattā*), which transcends the Accumulation-flow in which Volitional clinging and grasping for permanence constitute the passage of time for "you" in "the world." Because this *form* is characterized by the "death" of the substance-illusions to which the comprehensive-ideas of "the world" and "the self" refer, this form of be-ing may be called "living in the light of death."

§3 *Present(-)ing in the Light of Death*

This section will be presented from the first person perspective to help facilitate communication. There have been a number of times in my life when I have experienced extreme anxiety. It is not uncommon when children and adults are faced with impending or imminent loss, e.g. the death of loved ones, the loss of significant relationships, the loss of opportunities, or the loss of coveted possessions.

Notwithstanding any familiarity with anxiety, then, there were a number of events which seemed to converge upon me simultaneous not too long after earning my PhD in philosophy, including but not limited to the death of my father and the failing health of my mother. I remember feeling so anxious that I became sincerely concerned that I might have a cardiac event.

I had a realization in the midst of all the anxiety. My mind was, of course, filled with thoughts of death and loss. These words came to me, characterizing my realization: "*This is the me that will die.*" I sincerely thought I was going to have a heart attack, and the thought of it increased, rather than decreased, my anxiety. On the one hand, it seems appropriate to insert all the Western "existential" concerns here for an "authentic self," e.g. what would I want to do if in fact I don't die right now; have I been living my life in such a way that were I to die right now that I could accept this being the end of my life. On the other hand, as I thought of the cessation of whatever worldly identity I may have, I genuinely wondered: If *this* is the me that will die, what is *this*?

I think the value of the question is found in its calling substantiality into question. Though it is difficult to put into words, the "discovery" of the "me that will die" caused me to wonder if in some way I had already died. It is interesting to note here, as we will discuss later, that it is a samurai technique to envision one's own death, so as to invoke experiences of the type I am describing. One more anecdote, before we conclude the thought.

About eleven years before I concluded my PhD, I was swimming off the coast of Mexico. I had some sort of floatation device with me, so I felt pretty comfortable and safe. However, a large wave somehow moved me into the pull of an undertow. I still remember being surprised by the strength of the force. I was resting on the floatation device as if at the edge of a pool, so it was under my arms. Suddenly I was pulled under the water with such violence that I couldn't maintain a grip on the floatation device, no matter how I tried to cling to it.

My first time through the cycle of the undertow my focus seemed to be on the fact that the floatation device completely slipped away from me, and I lost track of it. As I came back up out of the water, my focus shifted to the fact that the undertow was overpowering me. I still remember seeing people on the shore and wondering if someone might help me. Of course as I was pulled under again I held my breath and began to realize that I needed to get into rhythm with the force of the undertow, if I wanted to live. I remember thinking next that I would "push off" from the bottom, since I thought I could feel the bottom – I was probably in about 10 feet of water.

As my foot made contact with the bottom, my attempt to push off was completely unsuccessful. The bottom wasn't solid enough. I evidently had been fighting the undertow, as my muscles began to feel fatigued, and my thoughts then shifted to the fact that I might drown. It is interesting to me in hindsight that I didn't think about not being able to live anymore as much as I thought about other people who would have to live without my help. I remember thinking something to myself like, "If this is how it has to be, then I accept it," and I relaxed. Evidently because I was no longer fighting the force of the undertow, it was able to throw me farther than it had been previously throwing me, and I was able to make progress toward the shore.

When we realize "the me that will die," or (more philosophically accurate) the be-ing that will cease to be when I die, then it is as if we have accomplished an awareness – a kind of mindfulness – in regard to the non-substantiality of "the world." Our focus is no longer on what we believe we may cling to in "the world." Rather, it is as if we are grasping for anything to cling to that is not impermanent. On the one hand, though it may not be our immediate concern, if we are in fact about to die, it is still true that we have accomplished a kind of freedom from "the world." That is, insofar as we are not clinging to it with our last drop of vitality, we have turned away from "the world" of materiality and material-based Accumulations.

On the other hand, then, we can ask, what is happening when I "fall out of the form" of liberation and am distracted from awareness of the be-ing that will cease to be when I die? In Buddhist terminology, it is as if we are "re-born" into one of the "karmic realms" of "samsara." Thus, as we shall see, the awareness associated with "living in the light of death," i.e. remaining "awake" in the face of attractive Accumulations, is therefore a kind of liberation from the undertow of karma's cycling.

Present-ing in the light of death, then, means remaining mindful that when death comes, it will be a "now" when it arrives. Thus, sustaining the realization of the non-substantiality of "the self" is tantamount to remaining mindful of dying in every moment, i.e. "living in the light of death." In the words of Zen master Shunryu Suzuki, "Our life and death are the same thing. When we realize this fact we have no fear of death anymore, and we have no actual difficulty in our life." (Suzuki, 2011: 83). Each moment of life is a moment of death. This is non-substantiality in the flow of impermanence.

§4 *The View from Now(-)here*

Are you able to see your experience in the present moment as if thoughts of "the past" and "the future" are coming solely from your mind? Just as we can separate the first of the Five Aggregates (Material Forms) from the next three Accumulations (i.e. the "mental factors" of Feelings, Recognition, and Volitional Formations), so too we can understand the meaning or identity of the mental factor Accumulations as originating from the mind *in the present moment.* On the one hand, what we are trying to *Recognize* is the fact that: if we take the Material Forms as that which makes a moment real, then the only moment which is real is the one presently constituted through *Contact* with the Material Forms. This insight may disrupt clinging to identifications with "the past" or "the future" by emphasizing their present unreality, i.e. illusory nature.

On the other hand, disrupting your habitual form(s) of clinging is a step toward waking up to the only moment that is (Materially) real. A mantra suitable for passing through this gate may be: "I am only truly here now." Repeating this over and over throughout the day helps "keep one awake." Of course, this is not the "highest mantra" because it assumes the substantiality of "the self" as it says "I." However, it works quite well to stop the kind of "dreaming" that hovers about clinging in the present moment. To put it in goal-oriented language: we are trying to shift awareness *from* the point of view of the ego, which clings to, and is conditioned by the clinging to, the Accumulations *to* the point of view of awareness itself, i.e. Zen.

From the point of view of Zen, then, in this moment it is as if you are already dead, or at least it is as if you have experienced "ego-death." Though experiential awareness of this idea may at first be frightening, do not be frightened. Rather, notice the calmness to which the insight points. Why may this be called "ego-death"? Insofar as the ego is that which may be said to direct Volitional Formations and be associated with the dream of past and future materiality, then disrupting its capacity to direct interpretations of the Accumulations and sustain the "dreams" of past and future with its clinging, it is as if the ego momentarily dies.

Buddhism has a standardized way to discuss this shift of point of view to awareness itself. "Buddhahood," complete Enlightenment, is described in terms of the "Trikāya-doctrine," i.e. the Three Kāyas (bodies). "These three aspects of complete Enlightenment are known as the Dharmakāya, Sambhogakāya and Nirmanakāya."

(Rinpoche, 1986: 36). The Trikāya-doctrine, discussed in the sutra known as *Discourse of the Explanation of the Profound Secrets* (*Sandhinirmocana Sutta*) and systematized by the Yogācāra School of Mahāyāna Buddhism, characterizes the manifestations of Buddhahood, (aka "complete Enlightenment"), as the "Dharma-body" (or "Truth Body"), the "Enjoyment-body" (or "Great Realization of Timeless Communication"), and the "Transformation-body" (or "Created-Phenomenal Body"), respectively (cf. Rinpoche, 1986: 36-7; cf. Thondup, 1996: 50; cf. Evans-Wentz, 1960: 10-11).

If we are to understand individual human existence (or our present existential situation) in terms of Trikāya-theory, then the following may be helpful.

> The mind's quality of being in essence empty corresponds to the Dharmakāya. Its clear nature corresponds to the Sambhogakāya, and its quality of unimpeded manifestation corresponds to Nirmanakāya. These qualities, which express the basic nature of mind, are what we term Buddhahood. (Rinpoche, 1986: 36).

Further, we are specifically interested in the Dharmakāya in that it refers to the shift of point of view to Zen, i.e. awareness itself, or "the view from no(-)where." I like this locution, not only because it articulates the point of view temporally but also because it fits so well in the locution: "The no(-)where of now(-)here."

Depending, then, upon how we contextualize the idea, the Dharmakāya may be described in multiple ways. For instance, "there are the traditional references to the Twenty-one Flawless Aspects of the Dharmakāya that represent a state of mind *not subject to change* or degeneration [emphasis added]." (Ibid). Further, in terms of temporality, Dharmakāya is reminiscent of "Kairos."

> There is an omnipresent aspect, in that the Dharmakāya pervades both samsara and Nirvana. There is also the permanent quality, because the Dharmakāya is beyond form, beyond all limiting characteristics, and has no origination or cessation; being beyond dualistic

or conceptual frameworks, it is without
highness, lowness, happiness, sadness, or any
kind of change. (Rinpoche, 1986: 36-7).
Importantly, "the Dharmakāya's unchangeable nature [is]
subject neither to degeneration, exhaustion, nor
impairment." (Rinpoche, 1986: 37).

To conclude, because our present existential
situation (this phrase is preferable to "embodiment"), when
understood in terms of Dharmakāya-theory, reveals the
activities of our mind and body as taking place within the
three manifestations of Buddhahood, it becomes possible
for us to understand the shift to the awareness that
conditioned our ego-based interpretations of existence
prior to the shift in awareness to "part of the Buddha." If
we think of it in these terms, then we are able to
understand the "enlightenment" associated with the shift
of awareness as a kind of "becoming Buddha." Remember,
"Buddha" means "awake." Put another way, this process
may be characterized in Western terms; what we are doing
is taking "non-substantiality" as a regulative idea (cf.
Scalambrino, 2015a).

Notice, then, that the "light" of "en-*light*-en-ment"
may be understood in a twofold way. First, it may be
understood as the "light of death," in that shifting the
experiential point of view *from* the karma-based-clinging-
to-Accumulations *to* the "light" that conditions our ego-
based interpretations of the Accumulations constitutes
ego-death. Second, the point of view of the light of
Dharmakāya is the view from no(-)where, and as the view
from no(-)where it transcends change, including the
temporal-material-flow in which we experience "our"
bodies and "our" physical death. Thus, insofar as the ego-
death in Sambhogakāya dispels an illusory relation to the
phenomena of embodiment in Nirmanakāya, then the
substantial self, which only existed as illusion prior to its
dispelling, dies. Because the Accumulations continue in
Nirmanakāya "we" have not yet (physically) "died,"
however, we are now "living in the light of death."

II.
Waking in the Stream

"The enlightened person is some perfect, desirable character,
for himself and for others. Buddha wanted to find out how
human beings develop this ideal character –
how various sages in the past became sages."
~Shunryu Suzuki, *Zen Mind, Beginner's Mind.*
(2011: 40-41).

§5 *Japanese Philosophy*
There are multiple ways to understand the meaning
of the term "Buddha." It literally means "awake," and its
traditional three definitions are:
> (1) "The first person of the Triratna. (2) The
> highest degree of saintship, Buddhaship. (3)
> Every intelligent person who has broken through
> the bondage of sense, perception and self, knows
> the utter unreality of all phenomena, and is
> ready to enter Nirvana." (Eitel, 1904: 36-37).

So, to be clear, I do not see Christianity and Buddhism as
mutually exclusive. Moreover, it is possible to "achieve"
Buddhist "enlightenment" through meditation practices
and still be a Christian.

The following are traditional divisions and names
for Japanese historical periods:
(538-710) Asuka Period,
(710-794) Nara Period,
(794-1185) Heian Period,
(1185-1336) Kamakura Period,
(1336-1573) Muromachi (aka Ashikaga) Period,
(1573-1603) Azuchi-Momoyama Period,
(1603-1867) Edo (aka Tokugawa) Period.

It was during the Asuka Period that Buddhism was
introduced to Japan from India through China. Prior to the
introduction of Buddhism, the Japanese did not have a
name for their "religion," which was later named "Shintō."

The idea, then, is that Shintōism was essentially an "animism" and, as such, included the practice of shamanistic techniques associated with harnessing the magical spiritual power pervading the universe. Ultimately, combining Shintōism with Yogic techniques from India, the Buddhist concern for "enlightenment," and the Daoist (Taoist) notion of "the Way" may be seen as culminating in the theory and practice of Zen Buddhism.

> Like the ancient techniques of shamanism, the beginnings of Yoga are shrouded in the darkness of the past. But unlike shamanic techniques, which aim at magical powers and ecstatic states, Yoga uses meditation and structured spiritual exercises in order to free oneself from the conditions of earthly existence. And while primitive shamanic elements have found their way into Yoga in a variety of forms, they have never been essential to the concerns of Yoga. (Dumoulin, 1988: 13-14; cf. Fischer, 1971).

Practically speaking, body postures, rhythmic breathing, and concentration having discernible results on vitality and associated with "de-stressing" and tranquility, were mixed with Shintōism and sharpened by the theory and practice found in Buddhism and Daoism culminating in Japanese Zen.

i. *Shintōism & Buddhism*

I continually find it fascinating that spiritual reality for the early Japanese people was so obvious that no "religion" was constructed for its revelation. In other words, the spiritual understanding of reality and beliefs regarding spiritual nature were so pervasive that – in much the way that friends innocently and comfortably speak without using names – the early Japanese had no formal name for their "spirituality."

> The native faith more closely approximated a psychological attitude than a religion, since it represented the closeness of the people to the land they loved and the deities venerated were the personifications of that land in the form of

20

its stones, earth, trees and mountains. Until the arrival of Buddhism, the autochthonous [native] faith did not even have a name; it was only designated "the way of the gods" (Shintō). (Matsunaga and Matsunaga, 1974: 5).

The sacred spirits, or *kami*, were ubiquitous for the early Japanese; thus, contributing to their disposition toward life as if it were innately good. "Every existent was believed to have a spirit and a great number of these were considered worthy of veneration. Basically the *kami*, derived from shamanistic and animistic beliefs." (Matsunaga and Matsunaga, 1974: 3). These beliefs contained notions regarding "the qualities of fertility and growth, natural phenomena and objects such as sun, wind, thunder, trees, mountains, and rocks; certain animals and human ancestral spirits were also included." (Ibid).

Historically speaking, the Japanese relation to nature as composed of innate goodness may have deeply influenced the innocence of their attitude toward death.

Shintō cannot be explained by any form of deism. Theistic doctrines revolve about deities who create the universe apart from themselves or who control the universe or deities demanding worship and conferring or withholding salvation and some form of desired satisfaction after death. According to Shintō, divine spirit [*kami*] did not make the universe, but *is* the universe. *Divine spirit* does not control the universe but *self-creatively expands as the universe* [emphasis added], for to control means omnipotent mechanism while to create means to generate the new. Mankind neither worships divinity in Shintō nor requires salvation at the hands of an aloof deity, for man and divinity are the same. (Mason, 1967: 99).

This idea that "divine spirit ... *is* the universe" makes Shintō soteriology more compatible with theories of sustaining natural harmony, for example those found in Daoism, than with soteriologies which are more "final goal" oriented. Whereas the former soteriologies may view death as an event consistent with the overall harmony of nature, the latter soteriologies may view death as if it were an unnatural event or an event somehow in contact with the supernatural as non-natural, rather than seeing the supernatural as consisting of the natural.

After Buddhism entered Japan through China and Korea from India, its "interaction with Japanese culture took six centuries to complete, after which Buddhism became fully indigenized and distinctively Japanese forms of Buddhism began to develop." (Picken, 2002: 37). Though today it is possible to find extensive lists of "different kinds" of Buddhism, for our purpose here we need only keep the following traditional types in mind.

First, the one most associated with India is Theravāda Buddhism, which means "Doctrine of the Elders or Doctrine of the Elder Monks" (cf. Williams, 2008: 18). Second, Mahāyāna Buddhism, meaning "Great Vehicle," arose from within the Theravāda tradition and spread across Asia. From the perspective of the "Great" or "Greater Vehicle," Theravāda is sometimes, and perhaps pejoratively, referred to as Hīnayāna, or the "Smaller Vehicle" of Buddhism. Third, when Mahāyāna Buddhism mixed with Hinduism it produced Vajrayāna Buddhism, variously translated as "Diamond Vehicle" or "Thunderbolt Vehicle," which follows the "tantric," i.e. the esoteric or "uncommon," literature of Buddhism. Tibetan Buddhism is often associated with Vajrayāna. Finally, when Mahāyāna Buddhism mixed with Taoism it produced Chán (or Ch' an) Buddhism.

Chán Buddhism comes from the abbreviation of "*chánnà*" as the Chinese translation of *Jhāna* in the Pali language of Theravāda and *Dhyāna* in the Sanskrit language of Mahāyāna, referring to the Buddhist notion of "meditation" or "no-mind." Further, the Japanese pronunciation of "Chán" is "Zen." Thus, Zen may be understood as the Japanese reference to that which these other terms were all attempting to reference. Notice, then, that Shintōism is the component which differentiates Zen Buddhism from all the other "Buddhisms," even Chán Buddhism, making Zen Buddhism distinctly Japanese.

As we will see, the manner in which Buddhism meshed with various Eastern religions – especially Shintōism – produced the distinctively Zen relation to death found in the activities of the Zen monks, the samurai warriors, and Japan's haiku poets. For just as Shintōism saw nature as self-creating, Zen practitioners may see existence as auto-poetic. While Buddhism was

> deeply concerned with the problem of individual enlightenment in India, its travels north into China changed it radically through its encounter with the eastern Asian tradition of ancestral reverence and the values of Confucianism. Its cross-fertilizing with Taoism, for example, in China led to what became Zen in Japan. (Picken, 2002: 37).

The idea that should be emerging at this point is that despite being the Japanese version of Buddhism, Zen Buddhism may be understood distinctly, especially the Sōtō School of Zen. The ability of Buddhism to mesh so well with Yoga, Daoism, and even to some extent with Confucianism, then, made its distinctively Japanese version, i.e. Zen Buddhism, "the spiritual guide of the warrior (samurai) class, particularly because of its cavalier attitude toward death." (Ibid: 244; cf. King, 1993: 10-14).

What remains to be commented upon, then, is to what extent Shintōism influenced, and perhaps altered, the Japanese understanding of Buddhism, especially in regard to the Zen relation to death. For example,

> the Shintō doctrine of conscience – the god-given sense of right and wrong – was not denied by Buddhism. But this conscience was interpreted as the essential wisdom of the Buddha dormant in every human creature – wisdom darkened by ignorance, clogged by desire, fettered by Karma, but destined sooner or later to fully awaken and to flood the mind with light. (Hearn, 1966: 19).

Take conscience, then, as an example with which to understand the intricacies resulting from the mesh of Buddhism with Shintōism. On the one hand, it may be said that in order to not disrupt the indigenous spiritual beliefs found in Shintōism, rather than attempt to change them, Buddhism simple assigned them a place in the Buddhist psychology and cosmology. On the other hand, notice how in doing so, Japanese Buddhism enriched the psychology and cosmology of non-Shintō-meshed Buddhism.

The complementarity resulting from such intricacy, i.e. the way in which Zen Buddhism may be seen as a harmonious mesh of Shintōism and Buddhism, reveals itself in a double-enrichment for the Japanese people in the form of Zen Buddhism. In other words, just as Buddhism enriched Shintōism, so too Shintōism enriched Buddhism.

> One particular attraction of Buddhist teaching was its simple and ingenious interpretation of nature. Countless matters which Shintō had never attempted to explain, and could not have explained, Buddhism expounded in detail, with much apparent consistency. Its explanations of the mysteries of birth, life, and death were at once consoling to pure minds, and wholesomely discomforting to bad consciences. (Hearn, 1966: 16).

Moreover, the

> Shintōistic beliefs made man positive and aggressive while the life-minimizing, negative views of Buddhism contributed toward making him desperately fearless and bold. Thus these two spiritual elements blended curiously to contribute toward the formation of a moral code of the samurai, which later came to be institutionalized as Bushidō, the Way of the Warrior. (Seward, 1969: 11).

Thus, as will be discussed in Chapter IV, the meshing of Shintōism with Buddhism blossomed-forth Zen and the way of the samurai.

Of course, the common element regarding both Zen and the way of the samurai may be articulated in terms of death. For example, whereas Shintō considered the dead happy or unhappy due to the attention they receive from the living, Buddhism

> taught that the dead were happy or unhappy ... because of their past conduct while in the body.

24

It did not attempt to teach the higher doctrine of successive rebirths – which the people could not possibly have understood – but the merely symbolic doctrine of transmigration, which everybody could understand. To die was... to be reincarnated; and the character of the new body, as well as the conditions of the new existence, would depend upon the quality of one's deeds and thoughts in the present body. All states and conditions of being were the consequence of past actions. (Hearn, 1966: 16-17).

On the one hand, notice that whereas the Buddhist understanding of death may be characterized in terms of karma and karmic-re-incarnation as an explanation of the mysteries of birth, life, and death, the question of the relation between death and the extinction of "one's life force" or individualized-Kami is left unanswered. Here we hear and echo of the intricacy discussed above,

in Shintō, there is no spiritual extinction in death. The body's decay is the mark of divine spirit's [*kami*'s] failure to hold itself in a personalized material form for earthly activities; and is also a clearing of the ground for life's renewed experiments in progressive evolution when the body no longer can retain sufficient vitality for creative action. (Mason, 1967: 94).

In this way Shintōistic beliefs colored the notion of Zen as de-personalized individual Dharmakāya no-mind, insofar as such no-mind may be characterized as the awakening of "divine spirit" (*kami*) temporarily individualized in "a personalized material form for earthly activities."

Not only is this Shintōistic influence on and clarification of Buddhism instructive for a Zen understanding of Nirvana, but it is also instructive for an understanding of the role of Zen in the way of the samurai and the Zen poetic-involvement with such "earthly activities" as arranging flowers, making tea, and writing poems. For example, consider the following passage: "Flower petals fall, but the flower endures. The form perishes, but the being endures... the word 'soul' is nothing but an adjective modifying the force flowing among the whole of creation." (Takeuchi, 2011: 3). This passage reminds us of the Shintōistic understanding of *kami*, i.e. divine, auto-poetic, inextinguishable spirit, while hinting at the distinctly Japanese aesthetic of *mōnō nō aware*.

In fact, the self-creative (i.e. auto-poetic) nature of divinity (*kami*) in Shintō also influenced the Japanese understanding of karma.

> Shintō had less difficulty undermining the debilitating influence of the concept of life as unreality and illusion. In India, where [such a] doctrine has been most persistently emphasized, escape from unreality has been sought by expanding the individual ego into the Universal All, considered as the only Reality. Not sacrificing the self, but magnifying the self to infinity [(Atman)] has been the actuating desire. (Mason, 1967: 192).

However,

> In Japan *the influence has moved away from egoism toward self-sacrifice*, especially emphasized in the code of the Samurai. *The philosophy of life's unreality was interpreted among the Samurai to justify the offering of their lives for some cause...* Thus, the same conception of the unreality of individual life led in India toward inactivity through the desire to overcome all earthly desires, while in Japan it led to an intensity of action by pointing to the fact that if life were an illusion it could all the more readily be sacrificed for some worthy human purpose. *The primeval Shintō urge toward fruitful action must be accounted responsible for the difference* [emphases added]. (Ibid.).

Thus, understanding the meshing of Shintōism and Buddhism is necessary to understand the vital differences between Zen and other types of Buddhism. This is especially the case, as we will continue to explore, with death, and the idea of "living in the light of death."

ii. *Zen*

The goal of this brief section is merely to gesture toward the meaning of "Zen" both generally and specifically, and then to gesture toward the distinctness of Japanese Buddhism as it involves Zen. In general, Zen Buddhism may be differentiated from other types of Buddhism in terms of its understanding of death, karma, and enlightenment. Specifically, Zen Buddhism may be differentiated into two traditions associated with the sects or schools known as Rinzai and Sōtō (excluding the Ōbaku sect from consideration regarding Zen given its Chán-regressiveness). The primary distinction, for our purpose, between Rinzai and Sōtō Zen schools will be the former's use of kōan practice, abandoned by the latter.

Further, a few words may be helpful here about the organization of the remainder of this book. First, having noted above that the Zen (Shintō-inspired) understanding of karma, and now the Zen approach to enlightenment, differentiate Zen from other types of Buddhism, the remainder of this chapter on *the history and theory of Zen* will discuss karma and enlightenment. Second, the following brief chapter with its focus on *the practice of Zen* will discuss mindfulness and Zen as instructive toward elucidating "living in the light of death." Finally, the last two chapters will discuss *the presence of Zen* in the way of the samurai and Japanese haiku poetry, respectively.

It is often said that the person to introduce tea to Japan from China was also the person to introduce Buddhism. He is known by the name Eisai (1146-1215), and he is credited with building the first Zen temple in 1191 in Japan (i.e. Hōonji temple). Derived from Mahāyāna Buddhism, Japanese Buddhists could understand their participation in Zen activity as the same activity in which Buddha participated. As a result, it should be possible to obtain enlightenment *in the same way* as Buddha. In fact, for Zen the more accurate verb would be "to reveal or unconceal," rather than "to accomplish." In this way, it is as if the practice of Zen is itself enlightenment (cf. Suzuki, 2011). Thus, belief in "instantaneous" or "sudden" enlightenment distinguishes Japanese Buddhism.

27

Confidence in the possibility of sudden enlightenment, then, differentiates Zen from other types of Buddhism. For instance, "being aware of the discriminative nature of human language and all the inherent dangers involved in the attachment to words as well as the intellectualization of the spirit, [Zen practitioners] sought to transmit the experience of Enlightenment non-verbally." (Matsunaga and Matsunaga, 1976: 205). This notion of "non-verbal" sudden enlightenment may be used to directly contrast sudden from gradual enlightenment.

To put it into the form of a question, we might ask: What is the difference between Zen practice and Zen? Considered in this way, Zen practice may be understood as one of the "six perfections" discussed in Chán Buddhism. Further, in order to understand Zen as different from Zen practice, some commentators have referenced "the transmission of mind which the Tathāgata handed down to Mahākāśyapa and was introduced to China by the twenty-eighth Patriarch Bodhidharma. This transmission was outside of the expediences used by [Buddha] when He expounded the sūtras," i.e. this "transmission" provided a "non-verbal" communication or "direct pointing at the mind for the perception of self-nature and attainment of Buddhahood." (Luk, 1970: 9). Thus, Zen is said to be "all-embracing," and Zen practice to be one of the "six modes of salvation."

However, Zen practice and Zen are often discussed as interchangeable or used to clarify each other. For example, in regard to the question, "What is Zen?" Bernard Phillips famously noted,

> *Zen practice* [emphasis added] is at bottom the act of giving oneself, of entering wholly into one's actions. As this giving becomes more and more complete, one's practice and one's life both attain to an ever-deeper degree of integrity and reality. It is not sufficient simply to practice a formal routine. One must enter into the practice and become one with it, so that it is no longer an action performed by a doer who is external to the action... To give up the ego is just to abandon the position of exteriority to

28

one's actions and to be 'all there' in them. (Blyth, 1973a: 4-5).

Here it is as if we are encouraged to think of Zen practice as the attempt to accomplish a kind of single-minded absorption into activity with the absorption itself being Zen. Recalling the adage that Zen is "the beyond that is within," another commentator suggested, "Zen expects us to experience within ourselves that the suchness of things ... is beyond [the mind], and that no number of words can succeed in describing, that is, reasoning out, the what and why of life and the world." (Tesshi, 1967: 131; cf. Scalambrino, 2015a: 60). Recalling the de-personalized *kami* dwelling within every person, another commentator spoke of the "the spirit of Zen," such that, "Zen aspires to independence, self-mastery, freedom from every form of one-sidedness which means restraint and conditionality. (Teitarō, 1967: 138; cf. Shinshō, 1967: 50).

Finally, to the question, "What is Zen?" here is a response from Daisetz Teitarō Suzuki:

Zen in its essence is the art of seeing into the nature of one's own being, and it points the way from bondage to freedom. By making us drink right from the fountain of life, it liberates us from all the yokes under which we finite beings are usually suffering in this world. We can say that Zen liberates all the energies properly and naturally stored in each of us, which are in ordinary circumstances cramped and distorted such that they find no adequate channel for activity. (Suzuki, 2006: 3).

Notice, again, how this description of Zen sounds as if it were describing the realization of the *kami* animating all beings, such that the realization *liberates* the individual. To say that Zen is "the beyond that is within" is to emphasize that it is not what you think about it; rather, Zen is the no-mind, beyond mind, which (regarding the individual) is the condition for the possibility of the individual to conceptually think about Zen. Thus, Zen is not what you think about it, rather it is that which is the condition for what you think about it.

§6 *Karma; Re-birth; Bodhisattva*

Of all that may be said regarding Karma and Re-birth, a basic understanding is sufficient for our purpose here, which is primarily to clarify other concepts discussed in this book. Karma may be understood in general as referring to "action," or specifically as a "Natural Law of Causation." Further, it is helpful to divide the study of karma in two ways. First, karma understood as (x) a cosmological principle; (y) a psychological principle; (z) a moral principle. Second, karma understood in terms of the Five Aggregates, and when we understand it in terms of the Five Aggregates, it is important to make the distinction between the Material Forms and the "Mental Factors" Accumulations, especially recalling the fourth's labels: "Accumulated Volitions Shaping Aggregates" or "Karmic Fabrications."

Just like "You reap what you sow" or "What goes around comes around," the study of karma as a principle invariably brings in temporal terms. "Buddha" is quoted as saying, "To understand your previous actions look at your present life; to understand your future life look at your present actions." (Quoted in Rinpoche, 1986: 164). This type of understanding may be applied to karma as a cosmological, psychological, and moral principle.

Before explaining each of the principles at a great depth, consider karma in terms of the Five Aggregates. Karma, as the Natural Causal Law, may be understood as applying to the Material Forms, i.e. Earth, Water, Fire and Wind. In this way, their presence to, and for, potential clinging is a law-like presence. They combine in specific ways, producing specific effects, etc. Beyond this, the Accumulations referred to as "Mental Factors," i.e. Feeling, Recognition, and Volitional Formations, may also be thought of as having a law-like presence. Again, they can only combine and cling in specific ways, producing specific effects, etc. In this way we can use these two different ways of studying karma to clarify each other. Therefore, in relation to the Material Forms karma may be understood as a cosmological principle; in relation to the Mental Factors, a psychological principle, and in relation to them both a moral principle.

i. *Bhava-Chakra, Samsara, Nirvana*

A distinction needs to be made between Re-birth and Re-incarnation. Whereas Re-Incarnation refers to re-embodiment after disembodiment, it necessarily includes theory regarding "past lives." However, Re-birth need not include discussion of "past lives." For example, superficially Re-birth may even be understood in terms of acquiring a new lifestyle, status or position. This distinction is also important because it removes one of the conceptions that make Buddhism and Christianity seem mutually exclusive, i.e. Christians don't believe in Re-incarnation. The second (which should already have been removed at this point) is the misconception that Buddha is God. If anything, "Buddha" would be a name for "the Holy Spirit."

Recalling the discussion above in regard to "remaining awake" and remaining mindful of Dharmakāya, Buddhism enumerates Twelve Nidānas, which may be understood as accounting for "continual Re-birth," and "continual Re-birth" here means: *either* moving from one Accumulated configuration of existence to another without awakening *or* submerging into the stream of Aggregates and temporarily losing awareness of the Dharmakāya light. The Nidānas can be understood as working separately or in conjunction with each other producing a "cycle of Re-birth."

In terms of the "world-ing process" discussed above, we may say that clinging and attachment to Accumulations rooted in the Nidānas obscures clear perception of the Buddhist designated Three Characteristics of Existence, associated with all of the Aggregates: "impermanence" (*anicca*), "suffering" or "unsatisfactoriness" (*dukkha*), and "non-substantiality" (*anattā*). Thus, recalling the Four Noble Truths, it is often said that we "suffer" (*dukkha*) as a result of our relation to our karma. In other words, it is when our perception and understanding of these Characteristics of Existence are obscured that we hypostasize "the world" and "the self." Thus, misperceiving and misunderstanding impermanence and non-substantiality, we experience being-in-the-world.

In this way, the Twelve Nidānas may be understood as the factors through which one has an obscure relation to the stream of Aggregates. Because the content of Aggregation is in flux, it may be understood as a stream; in fact, Buddhists' characterize it in terms of continual re-cycling. In general, then, the world-ing process – as it is in itself – may be referred to by the term Bhava-Chakra. The Bhava-Chakra may be understood as the Wheel of Re-Cycling Existence (or the Wheel of Re-Incarnation). The obscure relation to the Bhava-Chakra, then, manifests attachment to "the world," and this type of be-ing is called "Samsara" in Buddhism (cf. Scalambrino, 2014). Samsara is a dimension of suffering (*dukkha*). The Bhava-Chakra is permeated by karma, i.e. karma is the law of its (re)cycling.

It will now be easier to explain what "working on our karma" means and how it relates to Re-birth. Recall from above the three aspects of "complete" Enlightenment: are: Dharmakāya, Sambhogakāya and Nirmanakāya. Grouping the second and third aspects results in a distinction between Dharmakāya and Rupakāya. Regarding karma, then, Buddhism suggests, on the one hand, performing good actions, i.e. Accumulating merit or "good karma," reveals Rupakāya. On the other hand, Dharmakāya is revealed by Accumulating wisdom. Therefore, just as the terms En-*light*-en-ment, Dharmakāya, Zen, and Nirvana belong together, the enlightened relation to the karma of Bhava-Chakra *is* liberation from samsara, i.e. "Nirvana."

Yet, a distinction should be made between "Nirvana" and "Final Nirvana." The key idea here is that even though one may experience Nirvana, it need not mean that they will physically die at that time. The term "Bodhisattva" may help provide clarity. Whether through the Accumulation of merit or wisdom (or Grace) a be-ing experiences "great compassion" and the wish to realize Buddhahood, then "bodhicitta" has manifested. "Bodhi" means "awakening" or "enlightening" and "citta" means "mind." Therefore, one who has changed the relation to Re-birth itself – by manifesting bodhicitta – may be called a Bodhisattva. This is an "ideal character" in Mahāyāna Buddhism. Moreover, when a Bodhisattva physically dies, it experiences Final Nirvana (cf. Scalambrino, 2014; cf. Goddard, 1932: 174).

Considering the following excerpt from the Udâna Scripture of Theravāda Buddhism regarding Nirvana may be helpful.

> There is that sphere wherein is neither earth nor water nor fire nor air; wherein is neither the sphere of infinite space nor of infinite consciousness nor of nothingness nor of neither-ideation-nor-non-ideation; where there is neither this world nor a world beyond nor both together nor moon and sun; this I say is free from coming and going, from duration and decay; there is no beginning and no establishment, no result and no cause; this indeed is the end of suffering. (Johansson, 1970: 44).

Because it is outside the scope of our purpose here, we will not discuss the distinction between Pratyekabuddhas and Samyaksambuddhas. Moreover, though we will come to understand that Zen Buddhism is critical of establishing "Nirvana" as a goal, in the context of our discussion of the Bhava-Chakra, it may be characterized as the goal of the Four Noble Truths.

Nirvana may be described, then, as characterizing the relation of liberation achieved by Bodhisattvas who, whether through Accumulating good karma or wisdom, manifest bodhicitta and recognize "emptiness," e.g. of "the world" and "the self" (cf. Matics, 1970: 20). If we look back to examine samsara, then we discover there are "Six Realms" into which one may be "Re-born" (cf. Śāntideva, 1970: 227). These realms are divided into "lower" and "higher." The three lower ones are – in ascending order – the "Hell Realm," the "Realm of Hungry Ghosts," and the "Animal Realm." The three higher ones – also in ascending order – are the "Human Realm," the "Asura Realm," and the "Deva Realm." (cf. Rinpoche, 1986: 27). Of course, Nirvana is liberation from Re-birth into any of Six Realms. One who "has thus gone" is called "Tathāgata" (cf. Goddard, 1932: 122).

Lastly, recalling that the *Bardo Thödol* (aka *Tibetan Book of the Dead*) comes from the writings known as the *Profound Dharma of Self-Liberation through the Intention of the Peaceful and Wrathful Ones*, it may be helpful to hear the following two comments uttered in the context of Re-incarnation.

> [S]o long as the mind is human, so long as it is individualized, so long as it regards itself as separate and apart from all other minds, it is but the plaything of *Māyā*, of Ignorance which causes it to look upon the hallucinatory panorama of existences with samsara as real, and thence leads it to lose itself in the Quagmire of Phenomena. (Evans-Wentz, 1960: 225).

Prior to providing the following block quote, the above commentator on the *Tibetan Book of the Dead*, clarifies that as "the false powers of the finite mind cease to exist ... this is called *Nirvāna*." (Ibid: 226).

> All phenomena are originally in the mind and have really no outward form; therefore, as there is no form, it is an error to think that anything is there. All phenomena merely arise from false notions in the mind. If the mind is independent of these false notions, then all phenomena disappear... (Richard, 1907: 26).

This quote comes from a book the title of which suggests an awakening to the "absolute dimension" or "suchness."

ii. *Palingenic No Self: Situational Karmic-Assemblage Pulse*

The term "palingenesis" comes from the Greek "*palin*" meaning "again" and "*genesis*" meaning "the beginning of something." (Merriam-Webster, 2017). Hence, palingenesis may appropriately be used to characterize Re-birth and Re-incarnation. The purpose of this section of the book is to provide a kind of summary, now that we have discussed both the notion of non-substantiality regarding the self, i.e. the Buddhist doctrine of "no self," karma, and the Bhava-Chakra.

Combine these ideas. First, we have no substantial self. Second, karma influences both the flux of the Material Forms and the Volitional Formations (which includes Feelings and Recognition). Third, karmic Re-birth is into

34

one of the Six Realms of the Bhava-Chakra. When we combine these ideas with palingenesis, the idea would be that in new situations, the illusory substantial self we are "re-born" as stems from karma. It is not immediately clear how often we are "re-born." The answer to this question depends on how one understands Re-birth.

If we understand Re-birth in terms of karmic-situations, then it would be as if our "self" were pulsing re-born in every new situation. If we understand Re-birth in terms of momentariness, then with every passing moment, we are re-born. However we understand the palingenic cycle of Re-birth, given the non-substantiality of "the self," it is as if the reciprocal nature between the karma of the Material Forms and the Volitional Formations of the palingenic pulse provides a kind of "karma mask" for the no self. In the context of the no self that is "re-born," then, identity is a "karma mask." With this face, we "look out" through a "karma mask."

It is interesting to note how the idea of a karmic assemblage pulse relates to practice, e.g. as reflected in the insight expressed by this book's first epigraph – a famous quote from a samurai "manual" –

> There is surely nothing other than the single purpose of the present moment... If one fully understands the present moment, there will be nothing else to do, and nothing else to pursue. (Yamamoto, 2011: 76).

Notice, it is as if the single-minded focus on the situation facilitates enlightenment. For example, in terms of gradual enlightenment by accumulating "good karma" and not accumulating "bad karma," or in terms of sudden enlightenment, it is as if such a focus allows for insight into the non-substantiality of the moment and situation.

§7 *What is Enlightenment?*

Though it is technically incorrect, from within a practical perspective, to speak of the "goal" of Zen, many scholars, from a theoretical perspective, speak in ways similar to the following characterization:

> The goal of Zen is to encounter the intrinsic fundamental nature of Enlightenment existing

within each sentient being, which is alternately termed *kenshō* (to discover the true nature) or *satori*. (Matsunaga and Matsunaga, 1976: 204-5).

Of course, as mentioned above, Zen may also be articulated in terms of Rupakāya and Dharmakāya. Moreover, reminiscent of Plato's "Cave Allegory," Tibetan Buddhist Masters have likened the Dharmakāya to the Sun. Thus, we may speak of the light of Dharmakāya, "like light rays from the sun," while its brilliance prevents its direct perception by humans. (Rinpoche, 1986: 163).

i. *Gradual – Rupakāya Light*

As the section titles reveal, the traditional distinction between "gradual" and "sudden" enlightenment may also be characterized in terms of the Trikāya doctrine. In regard to Gradual Enlightenment – like the accumulation of Good Karma – we will discuss the Buddhist notions of the Six Perfections and the Ten Fetters.

Whereas Shunryu Suzuki translates *pāramitā* as "the way of true living," it is also often translated as "perfection."

> The Sanskrit word traditionally translated as "perfection" is *pāramitā*. This is an ancient word whose origins are obscure. On one account *pāramitā* derives from *pāram*, meaning "the other side" plus the past participle *itā*, meaning "gone." From this perspective, something is perfected when it has "gone to the other side," that is, when it has fully transcended what it would be in ordinary lives. Others, however, link *pāramitā* to the term *pārama*, which means "excellent," or supreme," such that something is perfected when it arrives at the state of excellence or supremacy. But whatever its etymology, the word *pāramitā* soon became a technical term in Buddhist ethics naming the dimensions of human character that are most important in the state of enlightenment. (Wright, 2009: 6).

It is clear, then, that "the other side" within the theory of the Six Perfections is Nirvana.

As we will discuss in the next section, the Zen sect of Buddhism believes in "sudden" enlightenment; however, it is still a sect of Buddhism. Thus, the following Zen description of the Six Perfections suggests that when one obtains the Sixth Perfection, i.e. "wisdom," one's point of view regarding the other Perfections is altered.

> Our life can be seen as a crossing of a river. The goal of our life's effort is to reach the other shore, [i.e.] Nirvana. *Prajñā pāramitā*, the true wisdom of life, is that in each step of the way, the other shore is actually reached... *Dāna prajñā pāramitā* is the first of the six ways of true living. The second is *sīla prajñā pāramitā*, or the Buddhist precepts. Then there are *kshānti prajñā pāramitā*, or endurance; *vīrya prajñā pāramitā*, or ardor and constant effort; *dhyāna prajñā pāramitā*, or Zen practice; and *prajñā pāramitā* or wisdom. Actually these six *prajñā pāramitā* are one, but as we can observe life from various sides, we count six. (Suzuki, 2011: 51).

We have already discussed enough material to be able to understand the inner-workings of this shift in point of view. The shift results from the sixth perfection's wisdom which grants insight into non-substantiality. This, of course, may also be characterized as "ego-death."

> When we say that *pāramitā* means 'transcendent action,' we mean it in the sense that actions or attitude are performed in a non-egocentric manner. 'Transcendental' does not refer to some external reality, but rather to the way in which we conduct our lives and perceive the world – either in an egocentric or a non-egocentric way. The six *pāramitās* are concerned with the effort to step out of the egocentric mentality. (Ray, 2004: 140).

Moreover, it is the circumspection resulting from circumventing the ego in which one finds the Dharmakāya light of death.

Staying in the context of Rupakāya for now, however, notice it is possible to list the six "perfections" as if they were six character-virtues associated with "gradual enlightenment." The list is usually divided in two, since the second set of "perfections" are associated with adepts. The first set of three:

1) *Dāna prajñā pāramitā* – is generosity, giving, non-attachment;

2) *Sīla prajñā pāramitā* – or the Buddhist precepts, morality, discipline;

3) *Kshānti prajñā pāramitā* – or endurance, patience, acceptance.

The second set of three:

4) *Vīrya prajñā pāramitā* – the constant effort of ardor, the courageous power to "see spiritual endeavor through to its completion," or "striving untouched by the fault of discouragement" (cf. Wright, 2009: 138-9);

5) *Dhyāna prajñā pāramitā* – Zen practice, the equanimity of single-minded-action, or the no-mind unintelligibility of no self;

6) *Prajñā pāramitā* – wisdom, insight into emptiness and insight into the no-thing-ness of no self.

The Westernized name for the theory of Re-birth is "soul-wandering" (cf. Scalambrino, 2016b), and the Theravāda way of discussing the path of liberation involves Four Stages of Enlightenment with which are associated Ten Fetters which bind souls to the cycle of Re-birth (cf. Goomaraswamy, 1969: 101-126). Enlightenment, then, is traditionally thought to be gradual according to Theravāda Buddhism. The path of the Arhat, which is, at least analogously, the Theravāda version of the Mahāyāna Bodhisattva, begins with the idea of "entering the stream" after one is no longer "charmed with their prison" (Goddard, 1932: 113).

On the one hand, the Ten Fetters are divided into "lower" and "higher" and there are four (4) "stages" along the way toward Enlightenment. On the other hand, as indicated above, since the relationship between Enlightenment and Re-birth is such that the Enlightenment leads to Nirvana and the cessation of Re-birth, the Ten Fetters and four stages also refer to Re-birth.

The following standard list of the Ten Fetters derives from multiple sources:

    1) "Identity View" – Belief in Substantiality.
    2) "Doubt" – Doubt in regard to the value of morality.
    3) "Clinging to Precepts & Vows" – Sometimes called "being Dharma-ridden."
    4) Sensual desire.
    5) Ill Will.
    6) Lust for material-Re-birth.
    7) Lust for non-material-Re-birth.
    8) Arrogance.
    9) Distraction.
    10) Spiritual Ignorance.

Keeping in mind that we are in the context of Gradual Enlightenment, if we were to think of the Eightfold Path as a spiritual stream which leads to Nirvana, then when one is freed from the first three Fetters, one is said to be a "Stream-Entrant" or "Stream-Enterer," and subsequently a "Once-Returner," meaning only one Human Re-birth will occur. Further, the Once-Returner has reduced the force of Fetters four and five.

Upon being freed from Fetters four and five, the Once-Returner becomes a Non-Returner. Non-Returners are Re-born into the Heavenly Realms of the Bhava-Chakra. They exist there until the Final-Cessation of Karma. The Arhat (aka Arahant), then, characterizes the final stage on the path of having entered the stream toward Nirvana. The Arhat-level is achieved through liberation from all Ten Fetters. Having achieved "Arhat-ship" one is no longer Re-born in the Samsara of the Bhava-Chakra. This is often discussed in terms of "*cutting*" the Fetters.

ii. *Sudden – Dharmakāya Light*

Sudden En(-)light(-)en(-)ment has two different definitions. Sudden Enlightenment may be understood as "Reaching the truth directly without use of language." (Matsunaga and Matsunaga, 1974: 102). It may also be understood as "Reaching Enlightenment without establishing gradual stages of perfection, i.e. one thought can instantaneously lead to Enlightenment." (Ibid: 102-3). Because the Zen school's teaching does not involve the complexity of the

Gradual approach, it is sometimes considered "shallow." However, insofar as "Waking in the Stream" to Nirvana was the "goal" of Gradual Enlightenment, then, of course, a Zen-Enlightened Bodhisattva may come to understand the complexity of be-ing within the Dharmakāya light, i.e. beyond the ego-death of Nirvana, and in the "light of death." Despite any rifts among the disciples of Mahāyāna Buddhism, to be sure, "By enlightenment, the *Chán* masters did not mean anything short of actual attainment of *Dharmakāya* itself." (Luk, 1970: 9).

In fact, just as attaining the Sixth Perfection seems to manifest, what we may call, "a less fettered" view of the Six Perfections, so too a similar relation seems to obtain between the Three Jewels of Buddhism and the Trikāya doctrine. That is to say, Stream-Enterers may "seek refuge" in the Three Jewels, which are: the Buddha, the Dharma, and the Sangha. Whereas the Buddha refers to attaining the perfection of enlightenment and the Dharma to the teachings of the Buddha, the Sangha refers to the monks and followers of the Buddha to whom one may turn for help. The relation with Trikāya doctrine, then, is direct.

> The Uncreated, the Unshaped, the Unmodified is the Dharmakāya. The Offspring, the Modification of the Unmodified, the manifestation of all perfect attributes in one body, is the Sambhogakāya: "The embodiment of all that is wise, merciful and loving in the Dharmakāya – as clouds on the surface of the heavens or a rainbow on the surface of the clouds – is said to be Sambhogakāya." The condensation and differentiation of the One Body as many is the Nirmanakāya, or the Divine Incarnations among sentient beings, that is to say, among beings immersed in the Illusion called Samsara, in phenomena, in worldly existence. All *enlightened* beings who are reborn in this or in any otherworld with full consciousness, as workers for the betterment of their fellow creatures, are said to be Nirmanakāya incarnates." (Evans-Wentz, 1960: 12).

Thus, the Trikāya doctrine "symbolizes the Esoteric Trinity of the higher Buddhism of the Northern School; [and] the Exoteric Trinity being, as in the Southern School, the *Buddha*, the *Dharma* (or Scriptures), [and] the *Sangha* (or Priesthood)." (Evans-Wentz, 1960: 13-4).

Finally, just as the Zen school may be said to approach the Perfections from the perspective of having attained the Perfections, regarding Buddha and Dharmakāya, "The Zen school is also called the Buddha-mind school. It claims that ... abrupt enlightenment is possible by realizing the truth that 'the mind is identical with the Buddha.'" (Shinshō, 1967: 42-43). Be sure not to miss the word "realizing." That is, not just understanding the truth but "realizing" the truth. Realizing the truth may be said to alter one's experience of time.

> In buddha-dharma, practice and enlightenment are one and the same. Because it is the practice of enlightenment, a beginner's wholehearted practice of the Way is exactly the totality of original enlightenment. For this reason, in conveying the essential attitude for practice, it is taught not to wait for enlightenment outside practice... Since it is already the enlightenment of practice, enlightenment is endless; since it is the practice of enlightenment, practice is beginningless. (Dōgen, 1997: 30).

We discussed this above in Chapter One. Recall that the idea is that to participate in the *form* of practice is, on the one hand, to participate in a form the practice of which has no beginning. Connecting the light of Enlightenment with the "light of death," the time in which one practices is the phenomenal-time of this embodiment. On the other hand, participation in the form of the practice of Enlightenment is to *be* in that form as Buddha (was/is). This is why the Zen school, as noted just above, may say that "the mind is identical with the Buddha," and in light of the other points made above, the Dharmakāya, non-self, Nirvana, *kami*, the Tao, the Way of Heaven, the luminous-radiant-emptiness, Buddha, is the no(-)where of now(-)here, and, therefore, the *Kairos* of "outside" phenomenal-time.

§8 *What is Attachment?*

In order to understand the following quotes from Shunryu Suzuki's *Zen Mind, Beginner's Mind* keep the context of "no self" or the non-substantiality of "the self," in mind. According to Suzuki, "Usually when you do something, you want to achieve something, you *attach* to some result [emphasis added]." (Suzuki, 2011: 44).

> So just to do something without any particular effort is enough. When you make some special effort to achieve something, some excessive quality, some extra element is involved in it. You should get rid of excessive things. If your practice is good, without being aware of it you will become proud of your practice. That pride is extra. This point is very, very important, but usually we are not subtle enough to realize it, and we go in the wrong direction. (Ibid).

Why would not realizing it be "going in the wrong direction"? Because the karma of the "extra elements" which have *Accumulated* suggest substantiality to us. It seems like there is a "self" who is accomplishing that for which the special effort is being exerted, and the same goes for the suggestion that it is taking place in "the world."

Of course, "usually our mind is very busy and complicated, and it is difficult to be concentrated on what we are doing. This is because before we act we think, and this thinking leaves some trace." (Suzuki, 2011: 47). "From the Aggregate of Matter arise the creatures of this world, as of all worlds, in which animal stupidity is the dominant characteristic; and the *māra* (or illusion of shape) constitutes in all realms of the Samsara." (Evans-Wentz, 1960: 15). Zen practice cultivates "No Trace" or "not leaving a trace," so as to remain free from the Lower Fetters and the illusion of substantiality. *Māra* refers to the kind of karma-based "constellating" through *Contact* with phenomena which constitutes "extra elements" in activity. "If you leave a trace of your thinking on your activity, you will be attached to the trace... [and] if you attach to the idea of what you have done, you are involved in *self*[-]ish ideas." (Suzuki, 2011: 48). "What we call 'attachment' is just these traces of our thought and activity." (Ibid: 49).

i. *Relative-, Monkey-Mind: Casting Shadows on Action*

Reminiscent of a passage in Aristotle's *De Anima* and Kant's "Copernican Revolution," according to Suzuki,

> It appears as if something comes from outside your mind, but actually it is only the waves of your mind, and if you are not bothered by the waves, gradually they will become calmer and calmer. (Suzuki, 2011: 17-18).

This is described as "stopping" your thoughts or your mind; however, the word "stopping" seems too goal-oriented and active. It may be better to understand what happens in terms of non-attachment. "Many sensations come, many thoughts or images arise, but they are just waves of your own mind. Nothing comes from outside your mind." (Suzuki, 2011: 18).

Believing in substantiality, i.e. believing in a substantial "world" and "self," is attaching to the waves of mind and relating to experience from an ego-point-of-view anchored in the wave to which we are attached. This may be characterized in the following way. On the one hand, when experiencing from the point of view of attachment to a wave, that mind is called "relative-," "small-," or "monkey-mind." On the other hand, "If you leave your mind as it is, it will become calm. This mind is called big mind." (Ibid). Thus, Zen Buddhists speak of "small" and "big" mind; however, we should remember that they are actually the same, since in essence "small mind" refers to the waves of big mind. Hence, it becomes possible that you may "understand activity as just waves of your mind. Big mind experiences everything within itself. ... Whatever you experience is an expression of big mind." (Suzuki, 2011: 18-19).

It is important to remember that "We say 'big mind,' or 'small mind,' or 'Buddha mind,' or 'Zen mind,' and these words mean something, you know, but something we cannot and should not try to understand in terms of experience" (Suzuki, 2011: 127-8). What exactly does this mean, however?

> The big mind in which we must have confidence
> *is not something which you can experience*

43

> *objectively* [emphasis added]. It is something
> which is always with you, always on your side.
> Your eyes are on your side, for you cannot see
> your eyes, and your eyes cannot see
> themselves. (Suzuki, 2011: 128).

Further,

> You cannot project your[-]self as some objective
> thing to think about. The mind which is always
> on your side is not just your mind, it is
> universal mind, always the same, not different
> from another's mind. It is Zen mind. It is big,
> big mind. This mind is whatever you see. Your
> true mind is always with whatever you see.
> Although you do not know your own mind, it is
> there – at the very moment you see something,
> it is there." (Ibid).

Thus, just as there is no "you," there is no substantial self.
The illusion of a self manifests from attachment to a wave.
Necessarily, then, "the self" to which the monkey-mind
clings is impermanent, i.e. "dead" because neither alive nor
dead. In this way we can truthfully say that because "There
is nowhere to come or to go"; "there is no fear of death"
(Suzuki, 2011: 19). There is no self to die; what will, and
what needs to, "die" is the illusory hypostasized "self."

ii. *Ripple, No Trace, Flow...*

In terms of the Five Aggregates or Accumulations, it is as if
the Contact between the Material Forms and the Mental
Accumulations causes a mind-ripple. By not attaching to
the waves of the ripple, we do not create a trace of "extra
elements" in big mind. This relation amongst the
Aggregates allows for the Material Forms and Zen mind to
continue to "flow" unperturbed.

In this context, consider the words of the Indian
Buddhist monk and poet Śāntideva.

> My enemies – desire, hatred, and such like –
> are destitute of hands, feet, and so forth. They
> are not courageous, and they are not wise. How
> can I be enslaved by them? (Śāntideva, 1970:
> 159-160).

44

It is worth dwelling with these words for a moment. It is as if our attachment to the waves of big mind gives rise to an ego-point-of-view, which – despite wrongly supposing a substantial self – Accumulates the Feelings in the flow of the Aggregates.

He tells us, "the mind should be examined with the thought, 'Where does it wander?' ... one should not cast off the yoke of contemplation even for an instant." (Śāntideva, 1970: 166). Further, as is reminiscent of this book's first epigraph and as we will see emphasized in samurai philosophy, "Whoever, having been enlightened, commences to act, ought to think of nothing else. Insofar as this can be accomplished it is by means of applying one's entire being." (Śāntideva, 1970: 166). For, recall that the sixth of the Six Perfections, i.e. *prajñā pāramitā*, is the wisdom of insight into emptiness and insight into the no-thing-ness of "no self."

Thus, "attachment" may be understood, as "clinging" to the supposed "reality of a self." (Rinpoche, 1986: 129), especially insofar as an ego-point-of-view depends on be-ing "anchored" in a wave of big mind. Though it is illusory, the ego of small-, relative-, monkey-mind creates opposition between the wave and the water in which it is rippling. In this context, some Buddhists speak of at-one-ment as "atonement," i.e. reconciliation, with reality such that be-ing at one with reality may be understood in terms of "ego death" and atonement for karma and an absorption in the Dharmakāya, Buddha, Nirvana, "light of death." That is, "When you practice Zen you become one with Zen." (Suzuki, 2011: 49).

III.
Practice: Be-ing Here Now

"The one aim of those who practice philosophy in the proper
way is to practice death and dying."
~Plato, *Phaedo* (64a5-6 & 67d7-10).

"In my view there is no Buddha,
no sentient beings, no past, no present.
Anything attained was already attained – no time is needed.
There is nothing to practice, nothing to realize,
nothing to gain, nothing to lose.
Throughout all time there is no other dharma than this.
'If one claims there's a dharma surpassing this, I say that it's
like a dream, like a phantasm.'
This is all I have to teach."
~Linji Yixuan, *The Record of Linji*.
(2008: 12-13).

§9 *Mindfulness of Breathing*
This chapter is brief by design. It aims to
characterize practice as simply as possible, and gestures
toward a deeper awareness of practice, in the context of
Buddhist theory, without engaging in the depth of theory
discussion found above.

Original instructions for mindfulness of breathing
(*ānāpāna-sati*) were given by (Gautama) Buddha. The
Ānāpānasati sutra advocates for placing focus on the body
by focusing on breathing. However, being oriented toward
Zen Buddhism, this chapter primarily follows the teaching
of Shunryu Suzuki regarding Zazen.

Recall, "The Chinese character Chán (or Zen in
Japanese) is the equivalent of the Sanskrit word *dhyāna*"
(Luk, 1970: 9), which means "meditation." Mindfulness
may be likened to meditation such that meditation allows
one to see the fullness of mind in each moment, developing
a circumspection *in* which to "see into one's nature, and
not be moved."

i. *Zazen: Centering & Mindfulness*

One way to remember the value and meaning of meditation is to cross-reference it with the phrase "Be Here Now." This phrase was popularized by Ram Dass in his famous book: *Remember, Be Here Now.* Zazen may be understood in terms of Be Here Now, then, by recognizing its emphasis on posture and breathing. By holding the seated posture, we "center" on the body that is Here. By focusing on the breathing we become "mindful" of the content of the Now. As we continue to meditate Here Now, we become aware of our true be-ing, i.e. Be(-ing) Here Now.

Though different information may be found on the internet nowadays, while studying Buddhist documents in the 1990s, everything I found regarding Zen meditation pointed to the number five and for the following reasons, which I have experientially-validated. On the one hand, counting to a number higher than five lends itself to getting lost in the counting. On the other hand, counting to a number less than five lends itself to cycling too rapidly in the count, i.e. again becoming too preoccupied with the counting, which is rather like a finger pointing at the moon than the moon we strive to see (cf. Osho, 1994: 205).

We sit spine straight with our eyes facing forward and barely open (too open is distracting and if closed, then you'll "dream"). Holding your hands in the "cosmic mudra" form (cf. Suzuki, 2011: 8-9) such that there is a small gap between the tips of your thumbs; the point of this is that if you begin to lean too much your thumbs will touch and signal for you to adjust your posture. Ultimately, we just sit and breathe.

> When your mind is pure and calm enough to follow this movement [of breathing], there is nothing: no "I," no world, no mind nor body; just a swinging door.
> So when we practice zazen, all that exists is the movement of the breathing, but we are aware of this movement. You should not be absent-minded. But to be aware of the movement does not mean to be aware of your small self, but rather of your universal nature, or Buddha nature. (Suzuki, 2011: 11-12).

It is as if the posture is the enlightenment form for Nirmanakāya, the breathing the enlightenment form for Sambhogakāya, and en-*light*-en-ment itself as the awakening to be-ing. Thus, awakening to be-ing would be waking to an awareness of big mind or an awareness of awareness itself (insofar as awareness is the presence of big mind), or the luminous-emptiness of Dharmakāya.

§10 *Mind as Garden Analogy: What are Mind Weeds?*
What is a "mind weed"? The moment you *Recognize* that you were just attached to an idea, you are looking at a mind weed. If we think of the mind as a garden, then the mind weed is attachment, and we tend our garden by "pulling the weeds."

However, since most people are not concerned to notice when they are attaching to ideas, it is as if they are allowing their gardens to be overrun by weeds. Recognizing you were just attached to a thought is recognizing that you have just been "carried along" by small-, relative-, monkey-mind; it is as if you were playing "the shadow games" in Plato's Cave by chasing the illusions which manifest around the Accumulations – like shadows being cast on action by karma and the ego-point-of-view.

i. *Pulling the Weeds: The Attitude of Gratitude*
According to Suzuki, "weeds give nourishment to the plant." Thus, he recommends,

> We pull the weeds and bury them near the plant to give it nourishment. So even though you have some difficulty in your practice, even though you have some waves while you are sitting, those waves themselves will help you. So you should not be bothered by your mind. You should rather be grateful for the weeds, because eventually they will enrich your practice. (Suzuki, 2011: 20).

We should understand this attitude of gratitude in a twofold way. First, we may be grateful of the weed we notice, because we remember that we could not always recognize them. So, recognizing a mind weed should remind you of the progress you have made in tending your

49

garden. Second, since the weed refers to an attachment, and attachment to the non-substantial fetters us, then we do not want to attach to the idea that we were just attached to an idea.

In this way, Suzuki asks, "What is true zazen?" and answers: "When you become you!" (Suzuki, 2011: 68).

> When your life is always a part of your surroundings – in other words, when you are called back to yourself, in the present moment – then there is no problem. When you start to wander about in some delusion which is something apart from you yourself, then your surroundings are not real anymore, and your mind is not real anymore. If you yourself are deluded, then your surroundings are also a misty, foggy delusion. Once you are in the midst of delusion, there is no end to delusion. You will be involved in deluded ideas one after another. Most people live in delusion. (Suzuki, 2011: 69).

Staying non-attached to whatever "sprouts" in our "garden" is itself "pulling the weeds."

> We should just try to keep our mind on our breathing. That is our actual practice. That effort will be refined more and more while you are sitting. At first the effort you make is quite rough and impure, but by the power of practice the effort will become purer and purer. When your effort becomes pure, your body and mind become pure. This is the way we practice Zen. (Suzuki, 2011: 21).

He describes this as "our innate power to purify ourselves and our surroundings." (Ibid). Thus,

> you will find the value of Zen in your everyday life, rather than while you sit. But this does not mean you should neglect zazen. Even though you do not feel anything when you sit, if you do not have this zazen experience, you cannot find anything; you just find weeds, or trees or clouds in your daily life; you do not see the moon. That is why you are always complaining

about something. But for Zen students a weed, which for most people is worthless, is a treasure. With this attitude, whatever you do, life becomes an art. (Suzuki, 2011: 113).

In this way, the practice of Zen may be understood as living with commitment, loyalty, and sincerity. The attitude of gratitude constitutes a committed, loyal, and sincere relation to the Accumulations, especially upon Recognizing a mind weed.

§11 *Vibrant Awareness: Contact Flow(er)ing-ly Emerges*

Consider the following analogy in describing the Zen-relation to our surroundings, aka our immediate existential situations. Were you to be sitting in a silent room listening to headphones, it is possible to be "carried away" by the music. This may be like forgetting that you are even sitting in a room or that it is silent. Were you, for whatever reason, to remove the headphones, especially abruptly as if *cutting* the experience of the music, then you could *Recognize* both the silence of the room in relation to your previous experience and, now from the silence, having just been "carried away" by the music. (cf. Scalambrino, 2016a: 72). As one Zen master described it:

> Sometimes I take away man and do not take away the surroundings; sometimes I take away the surroundings and do not take away man; sometimes I take away both man and the surroundings; sometimes I take away neither man nor the surroundings. (Linji Yixuan, 2008: 7).

Thus, there is an even more adept-way to traverse the process of Accumulation attachment. According to Dōgen, "Only the buddhas and ancestors know the blooming and falling of flowers in the world, only they know that flowers in space, flowers on the ground, and flowers in the world are sutras." (quoted and discussed in Leighton, 2007: 105; cf. Scalambrino, 2016b: 135).

It is as if from "within" the *form* which reveals the Dharmakāya light, a process of "flowering" may be witnessed at the points of Contact involving Accumulations. When there is no attachment to whatever

51

emerges from the Contact, then, regarding such "ripple, no trace, flow," the skandhas of every moment are cherry blossoms flow(er)ing-ly emerging.

i. *The Suchness of What is Happening*

By witnessing, with an attitude of gratitude, attachment to Accumulations as the sprouting of the weeds of delusion, we cut off the deeper karmic-traces constituting the World-ing process. In this way, correcting two common prejudices against Zen Buddhism, Zen Contact is technically neither Nihilism nor Eternalism, as both are weed-ways of attaching to Accumulations.

Think of the Mental Factors among the skandhas (Five Aggregates or Five Accumulations) as a membrane. Contact with the membrane by the Material Forms (from our "surroundings") provokes a constellation-process. This process of constellating the Contact constitutes the root of the weed-like belief in substantiality. Remaining unattached even to the constellating process, it is like a full moon, witnessing the weed-ing process in the Dharmakāya light of death. Rather than appropriate or identify with the Accumulations or any "constellating" that may be taking place across mind waves, the emptiness conditioning the experience is revealed. The suchness of what is happening may be characterized by the rippling of Contact within a luminous emptiness.

§12 *Channeling the Light: Sincerity is the Way of Heaven*

Laozi famously said in the *Tao Te Ching* that "When sincerity does not suffice, it was not sincerity." Similarly, Confucius had the following to say regarding sincerity in his *Doctrine of the Mean*:

> Sincerity is that whereby self-completion is effected, and *its* way is that by which man must direct himself. Sincerity is the end and beginning of all things; without sincerity there would be nothing. On this account the superior man regards the attainment of sincerity as most excellent. (Confucius, 1893: 418).

In fact, Confucius attributes the capacity for a kind of higher knowledge, which he calls "foreknowledge," to the Way of Sincerity.

Thus, beyond not being "carried away" by illusory phantasms or attachment to Accumulations, sincerity seems to characterize the way of living in the light of death itself. Be-ing sincerely within the light of death is to live with the awareness of impermanence (*anicca*), and non-substantiality (*anattā*).

> The Bodhisattva's way is called "the singled-minded way," or "one railway track thousands of miles long." The railway track is always the same... So even if the sun were to rise from the west, the Bodhisattva has only one way. His way is in each moment to express his nature and his sincerity... *Sincerity itself is the railway track*. The sights we see from the train will change, but we are always running on the same track. And *there is no beginning or end to the track*: beginningless and endless track... *Just to run on the track is our way*. This is the nature of our Zen practice [emphases added]. (Suzuki, 2011: 38).

To Be Here Now is to sincerely Be, and to sincerely Be is to be awake as the be-ing partially constituting the Be-ing of all be-ings. Articulated in terms of Shintōism, sincerity constitutes the awakening of "divine spirit" (*kami*) temporarily individualized in "a personalized material form for earthly activities" (cf. Mason, 1967: 94), and, thus, continual sincerity constitutes the Way of Heaven.

i. *Living in the Light of Death*

Are you able to see your experience in the present moment as if thoughts of "the past" and "the future" are coming solely from "your" mind, now? If so, then you are able to recognize the potential mind weeds that might otherwise be a distraction from the railway track of sincerity. The seriousness that comes from sincerely be-ing, is not attachment to seriousness. Rather, it is the ability to be both seriously serious and seriously non-serious. To live in the light of death is not to be overly serious or morbid.

Rather, it is to be honest about human existence and to sincerely perform the actions for which one's existential situations call.

To live in the light of death is to sincerely live-out one's karma, while be-ing mindful of karma as karma; it is worth quoting Jung at length regarding this idea.

> the "giver" of all "given" things dwells within us. This is a truth which in the face of all evidence, in the greatest things as in the smallest, is never known, although it is often so very necessary, indeed vital, for us to know it. Such knowledge, to be sure, is suitable only for contemplatives who are minded to understand the purpose of existence... A great reversal of standpoint, calling for much sacrifice, is needed before we can see the world as 'given' by the very nature of the soul. It is so much more straight-forward, more dramatic, impressive, and therefore more convincing, to see that all the things happen to me than to observe how I make them happen. Indeed, the animal nature of man makes him resist seeing himself as the maker of his circumstances. That is why attempts of this kind were always the object of secret initiations, culminating as a rule in a figurative death which symbolized the total character of this reversal... Such was the case, at least, with all the mystery cults in ancient civilizations from the time of the Egyptian and Eleusinian mysteries. (Jung, 1960: xl).

Living in the light of death through mindfulness of breathing shifts the experiential point of view *from* the karma-based-clinging-to-Accumulations *to* the "light," as if no longer deluded that a wave is separate from its water. This reversal of standpoint in relation to the phenomena of existence – the no(-)where of now(-)here – dispels the notion of a substantial self, diminishing the fuel for ego-clinging to Accumulations. Though continuing to experience the material realization of existential situations means not yet passing through the event of physical death, "we" are *now* "living in the light of death," sincerely.

IV.
Samurai: Knights of
the Eastern Existential Tradition

"Throughout your life advance daily, becoming
more skillful than yesterday, more skillful than today.
This is never-ending." ~T. Yamamoto,
Hagakure – The Way of the Samurai. (2011: 67).

§13 *The Way of the Samurai is found in Death*
The word "samurai" is a variant of the word
"*saburai*," which originally meant "to serve or to be in
attendance." For example, to serve or be in attendance for
the Emperor or the *Daimyō*, i.e. "retainer" or "master."
Samurai are also known by the title "*bushi*," which means
"warrior." The way of the warrior, then, is literally and
actually found in death, since *bu* means "war," *dō* means
"the way" or "the path," and *shi* means "death." Thus,
"*Bushidō*," i.e. "Way of the Warrior," is found in death.
It is important to remember that Japanese family
names are traditionally listed first. In the following list of
names, then, Miyamoto, Yamamoto, and Inazō would be
considered Western "last names," i.e. the Japanese family
names. The primary textual sources used to construct this
chapter are: *The Book of Five Rings* (1645) by Miyamoto
Musashi (aka Niten Dōraku); Yamamoto Tsunetomo's
Hagakure – The Way of the Samurai (1716), also known as,
the *Analects of the Nabeshima Clan*, especially when
contrasted with the *Analects of Confucius*, and *Bushido –
The Soul of Japan* (1899) by Inazō Nitobe. In regard to the
historical periods of time under consideration, recall the
following enumeration: Asuka Period (538-710), Nara
Period (710-794), Heian Period (794-1185), Kamakura
Period (1185-1336), Muromachi (aka Ashikaga) Period
(1336-1573), Azuchi-Momoyama Period (1573-1603), Edo
(aka Tokugawa) Period (1603-1867). Importantly, then,

just as the Asuka Period brought Buddhism to mix with Japan's "Shintōism," so too in the Edo Period:

> the four main classes of warrior, farmer, artisan, and merchant were legally fixed as hereditary castes, whose lifestyles were defined by specific sumptuary laws for each caste. Below these four castes were two classes of outcasts, called the Polluted Ones and the Inhumans. Although wealthy merchants were able to secure marital and adoptive alliances with warrior families, and free people could be outcast for crimes, in general the four castes were kept distinctly separated. (Cleary, 1999: xiv).

Thus, insofar as, according to Shintōism, the governance of Japan was in the service of the "Way of Heaven" or the "Way of the gods," then the samurai were warriors in the service of the Way by adhering to the ethical code of *Bushidō* and by being loyal to their patrons.

In a chapter titled "The Individual in Japanese Ethics," Furukawa Tesshi speaking of the *Hagakure* rightly suggests "death" is a "multi-significant" term for the samurai. Noting, for example,

> In this samurai bible we find a famous saying: "*Bushidō to wa shinu koto to mitsuketari*" (Bushidō consists in dying – that is the conclusion I have reached). The correct interpretation of this saying will enable us to grasp what the Bushidō of the *Hagakure* means. The key words of the dictum "*shinu koto*" (dying) mean, first, "becoming pure and simple" in the spiritual sense... it is self-evident that "dying" in this sense is far removed from the so-called "dog's death" (Tesshi, 1967: 228-230).

Moreover, it is also clear that "the 'death' meant in this instance is not death in the ordinary or physiological sense. Nevertheless, it is equally indisputable that the word here means at least a kind of death which is the utmost limit of human existence." (Tesshi, 1967: 231). As a "multi-significant" term, then, "dying," according to the *Hagakure*, means first, "becoming pure and simple"; second, doing one's duty, ever ready to lay down one's life – concentrating upon one's task, taking all the responsibility upon oneself at the peril of one's life"; and, third ... "dedicating one's life unconditionally to one's master's service." (Tesshi, 1967: 232).

It is fascinating to think that, on the one hand, one's "master" could be understood as "Buddha" or "Big Mind" or "Zen," and, on the other hand, one's service along the "Way" could be filled with so much violence.

Though I am persuaded that the comparison between the samurai and the medieval knights of Europe can be misleading (cf. Morillo, 2001b), my use of the word "Knight" in regard to the samurai is intended to connote – beyond *Bushidō* as "chivalry" – a reference to Søren Kierkegaard's existential "Knights." (cf. Scalambrino, 2016a; cf. Graham, 2008; cf. Scalambrino, 2016c). In other words, the idea I hope to capture by referring to samurai as knights is essentially their relation to death. This relation to death was not generally found, however, with the Christianized medieval European knights (cf. Morillo, 2001a).

Samurai training began in childhood. Sounding very much like the "guardian class" from Plato's *Republic*, training began at an early age, beyond literacy, regarding physical and spiritual training and the study of poetry. Swordsmanship was called "Kendo" or "The Way of the Sword," and "The Way of the Warrior" was called "*Bushidō*" (cf. Adolphson, 2007; cf. King, 1995; cf. Turnbull, 1977). Whereas *Bushidō* was heavily influenced by Confucianism, especially its stress on loyalty to family and "master" or "retainer" or "*Daimyō*," samurai were standardly schooled in Zen Buddhism (cf. Sōhō, 1988; cf. Nukariya, 1913; Oyler, 2005).

There are "traditional sayings" often said of the samurai; by noting these we may gain insight into how such a calling was understood. Catharina Blomberg in her book *The Heart of the Warrior* provides the following list of sayings:

"*Bushi no nasake*", 'the pity of a samurai', denotes clemency on the part of the strong toward the weak. The Confucian teachings which so influence Japanese society stressed that while a superior had the right to expect subordination from an inferior, this ought to be reciprocated by benevolence on his part. Because of his absolute dominance, however, mercy shown by a samurai was all the more remarkable.

The saying "*Bushi ni nigon nashi*", in another version "*Bushi no kotoba ni nigon wa nai*", meaning literally 'A *bushi* has no second word', i.e. that a *bushi* stands by his word and never lies, eloquently illustrated the conception of samurai honor. ... [a samurai] would rather forfeit his life than break his word.

The vast superiority of the samurai is expressed with the utmost clarity in the traditional aphorism "*Hana wa sakura ni, hito wa bushi*", 'Among flowers the cherry, among men, the samurai', meaning that as the cherry-blossom is considered foremost among flowers, so the samurai were undisputedly foremost among men.

One must not forget, however, that the *bushi* were popularly likened to cherry-blossoms in another respect also, namely that their lives, while glorious, were apt to come to sudden ends. In a violent society which lived by the sword, where private vengeance was the rule, and where matters of honor were settled by means of a duel or suicide, the lives of the *bushi* might seem as evanescent as those of the cherry-blossoms, which one moment are in full bloom and the next scatter their petals in the wind. Even more evocative was the popular parallel between the camellia and the samurai. Camellia blooms do not wither, but drop suddenly like a head cut off with a sword. (Blomberg, 2000: x-xi).

Notice, the Japanese aesthetic of impermanence (i.e. *mōnō nō aware*), then, includes the beauty of strength and power, and in this way we may say that the beauty of the glory of strength, despite impermanence, does not "wither" in the light of death. Rather, the event of death itself is glorified as exemplifying resoluteness, even in the moment of death.

In examining the following passage from the *Hagakure*, it is instructive to recognize the difference between Aristotle's "Virtuous Person" and the virtue of a samurai. The sphere of action in question would be fear. Whereas Aristotle suggests moderation such that a deficit of fear is a vice, the way of the samurai is precisely edifying toward a lack of fear. That lack indicates an excellence for the masculine-minded samurai. The *Hagakure* explicitly prescribes such a relation for the samurai toward death.

> Although all things are not to be judged in this manner, I mention it in the investigation of the Way of the Samurai. *When the time comes* [emphasis added], there is no moment for reasoning. And if you have not done your inquiring beforehand, there is most often shame. Reading books and listening to people's talk are for the purpose of prior resolution. (Yamamoto, 2011: 69).

On the one hand, the way of the samurai clearly recognizes the value of territorializing the force of habit. It also seems clear that awareness of such value comes from insight into physical training and the power of controlled muscle memory. The martial arts, in many ways, stand on such value, including meditation in motion, e.g. Tai Chi.

On the other hand, it is as if – combining a phrase from Epicurus with a Kantian insight – because the event of death is not an event in life and because merging with the (habit) power of memory manifests a transcendental relation to the world-ing process and thus one's karma-flow, the samurai passes directly through the event of death. This may be captured in a more simple, though also more epigrammatic, statement by saying the living samurai has "already died" or is, at least, living in the light of death.

Above all, the Way of the Samurai should be in being aware that you do not know what is going to happen next, and in querying every item day and night. Victory and defeat are matters of the temporary force of circumstances. The way of avoiding shame is different. It is simply in death. (Yamamoto, 2011: 69-70).

The Eastern existential concept of "shame," especially as understood by the samurai, is interesting. For our purpose, we may simply say that it is more than a feeling. It is a feeling and also an accompanying alteration to one's karmic-flow. This is thought of not only in terms of how others see you, but also the kind of events which will subsequently be on your karmic-trajectory, so to speak.

Thus, though ultimately and actively Zen, the samurai awareness that it is in not attempting to avoid death that we maintain our virtue is reminiscent of the Daoist wisdom presented by Lieh Yü-k'ou (c. 400 BC). "To live and die at the right time is a blessing from heaven. Not to live when it is time to live, not to die when it is time to die, is a punishment from heaven." (Liezi, 1990: 127). The samurai, then, affirming the transiency (*anicca*) associated with discussions of Zen philosophy, should regularly say "That time is now." Thus, echoing an existential wisdom also found in Plato's *Phaedo,* "the Way of the Samurai is, morning after morning, *the practice of death*, considering whether it will be here or be there, imagining the most grotesque way of dying, and putting one's mind firmly in death." (Yamamoto, 2011: 80; Plato 1997: 64a5 & 67d7).

In fact, sounding quite like an affirmation of Kierkegaard's "Knight of Faith," the *Hagakure* notes, "Although this may be a most difficult thing, if one will do it, it can be done. There is nothing that one should suppose cannot be done." (Yamamoto, 2011: 80-81). Further, as if delineating how to accomplish a transcendental relation to one's "own" karma, combining the above insight with the insight of using the force of (habit) memory, the *Hagakure* famously notes,

Even if one's head were to be suddenly cut off, [a samurai] should be able to do one more action with certainty. The last moments of Nitta

Yoshisada are proof of this. Had his spirit been weak, he would have fallen the moment his head was severed. Recently, there is the example of Ono Doken. These actions occurred because of simple determination. With martial valor, if one becomes like a revengeful ghost and shows great determination, though his head is cut off, he should not die. (Yamamoto, 2011: 81).

The "revengeful ghost" reference is quite beautiful, philosophically speaking; on the one hand, it refers to the channeling of karmic-power; on the other, directly to the samurai relation to re-incarnation – to be discussed below.

Finally, the sense in which the samurai way resonates with an emphasis on honestly seeing one's own existence – especially by en-visioning one's own death and seeing the present circumstances of one's own existence in the light of death – may be seen from the following passages. First, "Whether people be of high or low birth, rich or poor, old or young, enlightened or confused, they are all alike in that they will one day die." (Yamamoto, 2011: 81). Second, "It is a principle of the art of war that one should simply lay down his life and strike. If one's opponent also does the same, it is an even match. Defeating one's opponent is then a matter of faith and destiny." (Yamamoto, 2011: 138). What is meant by "faith" here refers back to the single-mindedness of not fearing death. For,

If a warrior is not unattached to life and death, he will be of no use whatsoever. The saying that 'All abilities come from one mind' sounds as though it has to do with sentient matters, but it is in fact a matter of being unattached to life and death. With such *non-attachment* [emphasis added] one can accomplish any feat. Martial arts and the like are related to this insofar as they can lead to the Way. (Yamamoto, 2011: 138-139).

In other words, "when you forget death and become inattentive, you are not circumspect about things." (Shigesuke, 1999: 4). The "circumspection" which results from keeping death in mind covers the entire way of the samurai.

> When you always keep death in mind, when you speak and when you reply to what others say, you understand the weight and significance of every word as a warrior by profession, so you do not engage in futile arguments. As a matter of course you do not go to dubious places even if people invite you, so there is no way for you to get into unexpected predicaments. This is why I say you will avoid myriad evils and calamities if you keep death in mind. (Shigesuke, 1999: 4).

In this way, the above discussion may help characterize the origins of "what might be called a Japanese 'culture of death' among the *bushi*, the Japanese warrior class, a culture that emphasized the active seeking of death not just in battle but directly through suicide." (Morillo, 2001a: 242). Thus, Yoshimasa (1349-1410) notes "It is said that good warriors and good Buddhists are similarly circumspect." (Cleary, 2008: 18).

i. *The Vows*

The four (4) vows of Yamamoto Tsunetomo, listed in his book *Hagakure – The Way of the Samurai* (written from 1709 to 1716) are often affirmed as samurai vows in general. The vows are:

> 1) Never to be outdone in the Way of the Samurai.
> 2) To be of good use to the master [*Daimyō*].
> 3) To be filial to my parents.
> 4) To manifest great compassion, and to act for the sake of Man. (Yamamoto, 2011: 147).

Of course, just as the samurai were called *bushi*, the "Way of the Samurai" refers to *Bushidō*. Before discussing *Bushidō*, as a kind of Virtue Ethics, the following quote will help emphasize the sense in which – despite clear connotations of "progress" in the vows – the Way of the Samurai resonates with Zen.

> "A certain swordsman said when he became very old:

'During your lifetime training there are stages.

'At a low level you train very hard but can't master the art. You know you're not good, and people agree. As long as you stay at that stage you can't serve your master.

'At midlevel you may still not be able to serve your master, but you notice things that are wrong with you and also see things that are wrong with others.

'At a high level you are a master of the art. You can boast about it, delight when people praise you, and lament how others haven't reached your level. At that level you can serve your master.

'At a level somewhat higher you pretend to be unconcerned. People know you're good. This is where most people stop.

'There is, however, a level a step above, let's say, a superior stage, in the way of the samurai. When you go deep into the way, you realize there are no limits in the end. There is no point where you can say this is it, and you see starkly how inadequate you are. So you spend the rest of your life without even thinking of becoming accomplished or without thinking of boasting, let alone looking down on others." (Yamamoto, 2011: 66-67; This translation comes from: Sato, 1995: 293; cf. Scalambrino, 2015b).

Notice that as a kind of "existential character ethics" the vows and "progress" on the Way of the Samurai relate to being an excellent expression of the form of samurai, and "*form*" here means "commitment," "loyalty," and "sincerity" in the Way of the Samurai. The competition, then, is first and foremost with yourself. Your ability to have mastered yourself is evidenced in your combat and outward interactions with others and "the world."

The type of manly composure for which the Way of the Samurai calls is clearly reminiscent of our previous discussions of non-attachment and Zen above. Here is the *Hagakure* characterization:

> There is nothing so painful as regret. We would all like to be without it. However, when we are very happy and become elated, or when we *habitually* [emphasis added] jump into something thoughtlessly, later we are distraught, and it is for the most part because we did not think ahead and are now regretful. Certainly we should try not to become dejected, and when very happy should calm our minds. (Yamamoto, 2011: 147).

Of course, reminiscent of the Daoist insights noted above, the biggest regret of all may be found in *not dying*. As Yoshimasa notes speaking of cowards with "flustered minds," "Sneaking past the proper time to die, they regret it afterward." (Cleary, 2008: 18).

Of all that we could say about the above *Hagakure* passage, notice two aspects. First, there is a clear sense in which we are to be mindful of present circumstances in light of the future. Regret and shame are like branches, then, on the tree trunk of death, we want to chop it at the trunk (to turn a phrase from Pascal). Thus, living in the light of death is established through commitment, loyalty, and sincerity, and true courage and self-control exemplify the Way. Second, the force is ubiquitous, i.e. the force of habit. So, it is not as if we can sometimes relate to our habits and other times not. Rather, the force of habit permeates our existence. Thus, in this way, the force directed by the habit of living in the light of death supervenes upon us as if baptizing us into a community of knights.

ii. *The Sword*
It is interesting to note that the "ancient name" for a sword was originally "tashi" which meant "great cutter." The word "sword" came into use in that the original meaning of the word "sword" "was 'to come,' that is to say, 'to come to the proper place by cutting.'" (Mumford, 1906: 349). Further,

> the name "katana" was adopted ... in contradistinction to "wakizashi" (waist sword), that is, short sword. The latter is always characterized by the absence of ornamental

metal at the tip of its scabbard, there being no difference between the blades. (Mumford, 1906: 349).

The blades of samurai weaponry were measured by "shaku," 30.3 cm in length. These are the following blade-lengths:

Katana (long sword) – two (2) *shaku*, 60-73cm (23 ⅝–28 ¾ in);

Wakizashi (short sword) – between one (1) and two (2) *shaku*, 30.3-60.6cm (11¹⁵⁄₁₆–23 ⅝ in);

Tantō (dagger) – up to one (1) *shaku*, 15-30 cm (5¹⁵⁄₁₆–11¹⁵⁄₁₆ in).

There is far too much legend and folklore regarding samurai weaponry to discuss all of it here. An excellent resource, however, is Winston L. King's *Zen and the Way of the Sword: Arming the Samurai Psyche.*

In fact, both of the following quotes come from King's book.

The "secrets of metallurgy" are reminiscent of the professional secrets transmitted among shamans by initiation; in both cases we have a magical technique that is esoteric. That is why the smith's profession is usually hereditary, like the shaman's.... Here it suffices ... to bring out the fact that metallurgical magic, by the "power over fire" that it involved, assimilated a number of shamanic exploits. In the mythology of smiths we find many themes and motifs borrowed from the mythologies of shamans and sorcerers in general. (Eliade, 1964: 474).

Using the term "character" as a double entendre, King explained, "The character of the swordsmith, for good or ill, was believed to enter into the very nature of the blades he crafted." (King, 1993: 73).

On the one hand, for example, there was once an infamous swordsmith, Muramasa Senzo, born in the mid-fourteenth century whose swords were described as forged with "hammer blows from the heart of madness." "Muramasa was a man of irascible disposition and his swords gained the reputation of being 'thirsty for blood' – dangerous to own (inciting the owner to quarrelsomeness) and use (even cutting the owner)." (Ibid). On the other hand, some katana were forged by Buddhist monks. "Before the Kamakura Period ... swordsmiths were either priests of the Tendai sect of Buddhism or mountain ascetics called *yamabushi*." (King, 1993: 71).

> The Tendai sect, which believed that hard tasks and spiritual exercise were the basis of self-cultivation, adopted sword smithery as an ascetic practice. Tendai monks often chased [ornamenting metal] on katana they had made, designs associate with gods and Buddhas. These designs were presumably embodiments of prayers that their swords be as mighty as gods and Buddha... According to *Bushidō*, the katana defended righteousness and vanquished evil. In peacetime, the katana at a samurai's side would prevent him from harboring wicked thoughts, and in wartime, the katana would smite his enemies to protect him. Only the gods and the Buddha were more powerful than the katana. (Quoted in King, 1993: 72).

Similarly, when understood from the perspective of Shintōism, the katana was seen as a "kami vessel" or a vessel for nature spirits honed by forging earth with fire.

Finally, there is another way that swordmanship has been linked with Zen Buddhism. The following insights come from Yagyu Munenori (1571-1646). Recalling the Dharmakāya light, "Swordmanship agrees with Buddhism and is in accord with Zen in may ways. It abhors attachment, the state of tarrying with something." (Sato, 1983: 106). Moreover, "The concept of void [emptiness] is central to Buddhism. There are two kinds of void: false and real. The false void is the state where there is nothing. The real void is the true void – namely the mind." (Ibid: 94). The mind is thus a "void that moves," and the movement of such a void "turns into a mind that prompts the hands and feet to work." (Ibid). In this way, "The void is a code-word that is to be secretly transmitted. It refers to the mind of the opponent... To see the void... means to see the mind of the opponent." (Sato, 1983: 93).

§14 *Bushidō – The Way of the Samurai*

In order to present the following information in a perhaps easier for the Western belly to digest manner, *Bushidō* is treated as a kind of Virtue Ethics. We may take the following commentator's articulation as a point of departure,

> *Bushidō* was a complex code of behavior consisting of a wealth of religious and ethical elements. It dominated and determined the lives of all members of the warrior nobility, making them an exclusive group in society. For many centuries the rules of *Bushidō* were taught by example, transmitted from parents to children, and its precepts remained one of the privileges of the samurai. To the common people the *bushi*, although superior and remote, appeared as models worthy of emulation, especially where the Confucian virtues of filial piety and loyalty were concerned. (Blomberg, 2000: xii).

Further, despite influence from the

> Shintō and Buddhist clergy ... it was *bushi* influence which permeated Japanese society from top to bottom. From costume and manners to the decorative as well as the performing arts they set the standards, creating many of the values which have later come to be regarded as characteristically Japanese. (Blomberg, 2000: xii).

Again, though there were clearly Buddhist, Confucian, Daoist, and Shintō influences on the Way of the Samurai, in terms of practice and in emphasizing living life in the light of death, it is the similarities with Zen Buddhism which interest us most here.

Just like Aristotle's virtues, there are multiple ways to count the virtues of *Bushidō*. One may often find the number at seven (7) or eight (8). For our purpose, because we will count – though we will not discuss – "Fraternity" as a virtue like Aristotle's notion of "*Friendship* among the virtuous," we will count eight (8).

i. Gi – *Rectitude or Justice*

This virtue may be characterized in terms of commitment and resolution. "A well-known *bushi* defines ... 'Rectitude is the power of deciding upon a certain course of conduct in accordance with reason, without wavering; - to die when it is right to die, to strike when to strike is right.'" (Inazō, 1908: 21). As we may see by comparing the Japanese term with the term for the seventh virtue, Rectitude, i.e. Rightness, or Justice is closely related to Duty, insofar as our understanding of Duty derives from performing actions for the right reasons.

ii. Rei – *Politeness or Respect*

"Respect" is the better term here; however, because it pertains to an outward disposition toward others, politeness still holds. The idea here, and this is why respect is the better term, is that it is a relation to others based in merit. As the *Hagakure* has it, "Even when greeting someone lightly, one should consider the circumstances and after deliberation speak in a way that will not injure the man's feelings." (Yamamoto, 2011: 82). This virtue is related then to Aristotle's virtue of "nemesis" in that, according to Yoshimasa,

> For a person to be bad tempered is more disgraceful than anything. No matter how irritated you may be, at the very first thought you should calm your mind and distinguish right from wrong. *If you are in the right, then you may get angry...* It is a good thing to be willing to change when you're wrong. It is problematic to insist on thinking and behaving in a certain way, regardless of good or bad, just because that's what you've been doing. [emphasis added] (Clearly, 2008: 21).

iii. Yū – *Heroic Courage*

The reason it is helpful to modify "courage" here with "heroic" is that this is sacrificial courage.

The *Masters of Huainan* also says, 'When two people cross swords and their skills are no different, it is the brave man who will win. Why? Because of the seriousness with which he acts.' Victory and defeat are not in relative skill, courage or cowardice make the difference. The courageous are unafraid, so they're able to concentrate completely, without distraction. That is how they secure their victories. (Cleary, 2008: 215).

As the *Hagakure* explains, "In constantly hardening one's resolution to die in battle, *deliberately becoming as one already dead* [emphasis added], and working at one's job and dealing with military affairs, there should be no shame." (Yamamoto, 2011: 72).

As one samurai classic has it, heroic courage is beyond the commonplace conception of courage.

The key to the warrior's heart is maintaining courage. Courage means your mind and your mood do not get upset or lose normalcy. This is called being stalwart.

So the commonplace conception of courage as simply being unafraid when seeing or hearing frightening things is not complete courage. When neither normalcy nor emergency moves your mind, nor even sensual desires, when your expression doesn't change even if a mountain crumbles before you, you don't get angry even if people offend and insult you, you aren't fazed even by a major war, you're unafraid even when death is imminent, your heart is not discouraged by poverty and loss, you are not intimidated by people in high ranks and high offices, your mind is not distracted by trifles, you are not scared of anything, and you are unfailingly fearless and imperturbable, this manliness is called courage. (Cleary, pp. 138-139).

iv. Meiyo – *Honor & Dignity*

Honor and Dignity have something in common with Aristotle's virtue of modesty in that both seem to suggest a person is supposed to be honest about their own merit. As it is stated in *Bushido: The Soul of Japan*,

> The sense of honor, implying a vivid consciousness of personal dignity and worth, could not fail to characterize the samurai, born and bred to value the duties and privileges of their profession. ... A good name – one's reputation, the immortal part of one's self ... any infringement upon its integrity was felt as shame (Inazō, 1908: 65-66)

The sense of honor and dignity here is reminiscent of Aristotle's Great-Souled Person (cf. Aristotle, 2009: 1124a25). Whereas "the Zen monk and the samurai were distinguished by their manliness and dignity in manner, something amounting to rudeness" (Nukariya, 1913:23), the "morbid excess into which the delicate code of honor was inclined to run was strongly counterbalanced by preaching magnanimity and patience." (Inazō, 1908: 69; cf. Scalambrino, 2016a: 58).

v. Jin – *Compassion*

On the one hand, this virtue is reminiscent of the "Four Great Vows" of Buddhism:

> 1) However innumerable beings are, I vow to save them;
> 2) However, inexhaustible the passions are, I vow to extinguish them;
> 3) However immeasurable the Dharmas are I vow to master them;
> 4) However incomparable the Buddha-truth is, I vow to attain it.

On the other hand, this virtue is reminiscent of the Confucian ethical notion regarding superiors and inferiors, i.e. "while a superior had the right to expect subordination from an inferior, this ought to be reciprocated by benevolence on his part. Because of his absolute dominance, however, mercy shown by a samurai was all the more remarkable." (Blomberg, 2000: x).

vi. Makoto – *Sincerity & Integrity*

It may appear odd at first to think were everything in this book boiled down to one word that the word would be "sincerity." Absolute sincerity. The freedom of absolute sincerity, the excellence of absolute sincerity, for being absolutely sincere about what we are doing at every moment, would reveal an excellent harmony (cf. Suzuki, 2011: 38). Thus, it is worth quoting both the *Hagakure* and *Bushido: The Soul of Japan* here at length.

The following story comes from the *Hagakure* regarding sincerity,

> A certain person said, 'In the Saint's mausoleum there is a poem that goes:
>
> > *If in one's heart*
> > *He follows the path of sincerity,*
> > *Though he does not pray*
> > *Will not the gods protect him?*
>
> What is this path of sincerity?'
> A man answered [this certain person] by saying, 'You seem to like poetry. I will answer you with a poem.
>
> > *As everything in this world is but a shame,*
> > *Death is the only sincerity.*
>
> It is said that becoming as a dead man in one's daily living is the following of the path of sincerity.' (Yamamoto, 2011: 126).

To be so singularly focused on the present task, i.e. that one accomplish it or die working at it, is to excellently be in the moment; thus, it is life *sincerely* expressed in the light of death.

In *Bushido: The Soul of Japan*, then, we hear the following: "The apotheosis of Sincerity to which Tsu-tsu gives expression in the *Doctrine of the Mean*, attributes to it transcendental powers, almost identifying it with the divine." (Inazō, 1908: 56). The quote runs, "Sincerity is the end and the beginning of all things; without Sincerity there would be nothing." Thus, in terms of honesty, the samurai considered their word so important that for a samurai to give his "word carried such weight with it that promises were generally made and fulfilled without a written pledge, which would have been deemed quite beneath his dignity."

(Ibid: 57). In terms of Zen, the samurai may be understood as sincerely doing what "the Way of the Samurai," i.e. *Bushidō*, calls for *in each moment*.

vii. Chūgi – *Duty & Loyalty*

This virtue has been characterized as "homage and fealty to a superior." (Inazō, 1908: 74). This may be understood as devotion to a sovereign. For, "whereas in China Confucian ethics made obedience to parents the primary human duty, in Japan precedence was given to Loyalty." (Ibid: 76; cf. Yamamoto, 2011: 89 & 138). Samurai, then, are responsible for their actions and for not acting when they, according to the Way of the Samurai, should have. Inazō presents a nice contrast between East and West concerning Duty and Loyalty:

> The individualism of the West, which recognizes separate interests for father and son, husband and wife, necessarily brings into strong relief the duties owed by one to the other; but *Bushidō* held that the interest of the family and of the members thereof is intact, [i.e.] one and inseparable. This interest is bound up with affection – natural, instinctive, irresistible; hence, if we die for one we love with natural love (which animals themselves possess), what is that? (Inazō, 1908: 79).

The samurai were supposed to choose loyalty and duty over affection. In this way, sincere subjection to the will of the sovereign, then, characterizes the following of military orders and the courage to die in battle.

Finally, the virtue of loyalty may be seen in relation to Zen. The *Hagakure* expresses this virtue along a trajectory including family and courage:

> When [a samurai] is attending to matters, there is one thing that comes forth from his heart. That is, in terms of one's lord, loyalty; in terms of one's parents, filial piety; in martial affairs, bravery; and apart from that something that can be used by all the world.
> This is difficult to discover. Once discovered, it is again difficult to keep in constant effect. [I.e.]

There is nothing outside the thought of the immediate moment. (Yamamoto, 2011: 72).

More explicitly, Yoshimasa explained,

Being able to live in the world is due to the benevolence of the ruler to begin with... When people in society who should be in civil service demean themselves, thinking it won't be easy for them, this is a regrettably foolish thing. Having been born a human, you should aspire to surpass the masses and help other people, making it your pleasure to do your utmost for others, lifetime after lifetime, generation after generation. Since this alone is the purpose of the bodhisattva, if while an ordinary person your aspiration is equivalent to that of a bodhisattva, what satisfaction could be greater than that? (Cleary, 2008: 20).

Coda: The Dark Side of the Way – The Ninja

The interesting way the figure of the "ninja" (aka "Shinobi") relates – through Buddhism and Shintōism – to the figure of the samurai calls for some commentary.

[E]lements of ancient Taoism, practices commonly called magical or shamanic, seem to have entered Japan earlier, from both China and Korea. Taoist shamanism seems to have merged with its Shintō counterparts in Japan, particularly after being legally banned in the eighth century. Shamanic Taoism of the so-called Left-Hand Path, a sinister appellation also applied to an element of Tantric Buddhism, includes methods of demonic or magical warfare, brandishing destructive techniques based on mental or physical poisoning. This left-hand path, amalgamated with Shintō and Buddhist analogs, underlay the evolution of the lore of the *ninja* assassin. Events of ambiguous reality emerging from this tradition often mirror tactical use of insidious [hypnotic] suggestion to cast enemies into states of mental terror. (Cleary, 2008: 2).

What Cleary means here by "ambiguous reality" is not clear. However, research on Buddhism often reveals references to "paranormal" or "supernormal" "powers," which practitioners may "acquire" or "develop."

Regarding "Self-Mastery" according to "Early Buddhist Texts" Julius Evola refers to the presence of such powers as evidence "along the path of awakening" that "the Buddhist *askēsis* [self-discipline] does not move toward a state of nothingness ... to wait for final 'annihilation,' but that it is accompanied by ever greater degrees of consciousness, completeness, elevation, and power." (1996: 183). The clarification regarding the difficulty of understanding such "transformation" is worth mentioning:

> The problem of the extranormal and supernormal powers is connected with the view of the world. When nature is not conceived as an independent reality, but rather as *the outward form in which immaterial forces manifest themselves* [emphasis added]; when, further-more, one admits the possibility of removing, under certain conditions, the purely individual, sensory-cerebral consciousness of a man so as to allow of positive contacts with those immaterial forces – then... Free from the bond of the senses and of samsaric individuality, neutral, extremely balanced, this consciousness... [For example,] can directly realize the object whose image is evoked, by producing either telepathic knowledge, or objective penetration of the mind of an other, or, finally, vision of distant things. (Evola, 1996: 185).

Of course, in terms of the analytically-minded Western reading here, questions of "causality" may arise.

Interestingly, then, emphasizing the sense in which humans may become aware "not only of objects but also of the causal connections between them," one commentator explained "the Buddha claimed to have attained the sixfold higher knowledge. Its forms are:

> 1) *Psychokinesis* – This is the notion of "futural be-ing" from Chapter One. It speaks to "your" ability to

"move yourself" in different moments of time with your mind from this moment.

2) *Clairaudience* – This is the ability to hear two kinds of sound, i.e. human and divine.

3) *Telepathy* – This is the ability to know "the general state as well as the functioning of another's mind." This is described as "listening to the vibrations" while others are thinking in your presence.

4) *Retrocognition* – This is the ability to recall "one's manifold past existences... Dying there, I was born here," etc.

5) *Clairvoyance* – Knowledge, regarding Re-birth, of the dying and surviving of beings, – This is sometimes called "the divine eye," and it involves the ability to witness "the decease and survival of other beings."

6) *Extra-sensory perception of the destruction of defiling impulses* – This is the ability to "verify the four Noble Truths" of Buddhism (Kalupahana, 1975: 104-107).

Whereas through 4 & 5 Buddha was able to "verify the problem of rebirth," through 6 came verification the field of karma and karmic-rebirth.

Beyond, then, the fascination that discussion of these powers may hold for us, insofar as they may be weaponized, we may be looking at an enumeration of the "magic" and shamanic-power exploited by ninjas.

§15 *Seppuku: Samurai Suicide*

To begin, the word "*seppuku*" is the Japanese rendering of the Chinese characters for "cutting the stomach," thus nowadays we hear the more literal translation of those characters in the word "hari-kari." Commentators suggest the reason for choosing the abdomen comes from the belief that it represents "the cradle of one's will, thought, generosity, boldness, spirit, anger, etc." (Seward, 1969: 29). In a word, the soul was thought to reside, or be anchored, there in the body. When performing *seppuku*, a samurai makes a left-to-right cut into his abdomen and often a "second" or *kaishaku-nin* is present to "cut off" the head of the samurai performing *seppuku.* The cut was called the *kaishaku* and when performed excellently would leave enough flesh that the person's head would not roll on the floor.

i. *What Calls for Seppuku?*

As Nitobe Inazō eloquently put it in *Bushido – The Soul of Japan*, "*seppuku* was not a mere suicidal process. It was an institution, legal and ceremonial... [such that] warriors could expiate their crimes, apologize for errors, escape from disgrace, redeem their friends, or prove their sincerity." (1908: 105). It has been called the zenith or pinnacle of "self-control," and a

> mode of death ... associated with instances of noblest deeds and of most touching *pathos*, so that nothing repugnant, much less ludicrous, mars our conception of it. So wonderful is the transforming power of virtue, of greatness, of tenderness, that the vilest form of death assumes a sublimity and becomes a symbol of new life... (Inazō, 1908: 101).

In other words, "It was a refinement of self-destruction, and none could perform it without the utmost coolness of temper and composure of demeanor, and for these reasons it was particularly befitting the profession of *bushi*." (Inazō, 1908: 105-106; cf. Becker, 1990; cf. Bloom, 2005; cf. Picone, 2012; cf. Reuter, 2002; cf. Schulman, 1980; cf. Young, 2002). Moreover, "there is good reason to infer that the act of *seppuku* was associated with the austerities and self-mortification of Zen." (Seward, 1969: 31).

Traditional situations which may call to the samurai for *seppuku* include:

> 1) [origin of *seppuku*] to avoid being dishonored by defeat or capture
> 2) [*chugi-bara: junshi*] as a show of loyalty in the event of a samurai's *daimyō*'s death
> 3) [*chugi-bara: kanshi*] to protest a *daimyō*'s decision, aka "remonstration death"
> 4) [*munen-bara: funshi*] to protest an injustice, e.g. some dishonorable treatment by a samurai's *daimyō*

5) [*sokotsu-shi*] in lieu of execution as a capital punishment to avoid the shame of being found guilty of such crimes. (cf. Morillo, 2001: 248).

According to one of the best scholarly resources on *seppuku*, Jack Seward's *Hara-Kiri: Japanese Ritual Suicide* (1969), it was during the Muromachi (aka Ashikaga) Period (1336-1573) that *seppuku* was added to the previous two types of death penalty – strangulation and decapitation.

With the Edo (aka Tokugawa) Period (1603-1867), then, the following "five grades of penalties were instituted for the samurai class:

1) *Hissoku* – Contrite Seclusion. This Penalty was subdivided into three parts: restraint, circumspect prudence, and humility.
2) *Heimon* – Domiciliary Confinement. This was subdividied into two: 50 days and 100 days.
3) *Chikkyo* – Solitary Confinement. This was subdivided into three: confinement in one room, temporary retirement, and permanent retirement (until death).
4) *Kai-eki* – Attainder. Permanent removal of the name of the offender from the role of the samurai.
5) *Seppuku*. (Seward, 1969: 29).

Presumably, if the shame associated with any of penalties 1 thru 4 was too significant to carry, a samurai could perform *seppuku* as an alternative.

ii. *Martyrdom, Noble Death, and Karma*
It may be valuable to look at the definition of the word "noble" here. It means:

having, showing, or coming from personal qualities that people admire (such as honesty, generosity, courage, etc.)
of, relating to, or belonging to the highest social class: of, relating to, or belonging to nobility
impressive in magnitude or appearance ["illustrious, excellent, honorable"]. (Merriam-Webster, 2017).

Thus, as we have seen above, *seppuku* may be referred to as a "Noble Death" in that shame is the converse or reverse of honor. This is not as difficult a thesis to understand as the relation between suicide and karma or reincarnation.

The idea of a "noble death," then, seems to involve the notion of self-sacrifice or "martyrdom" in the sense of "witnessing" – in the case of the samurai – for the truth of *Bushidō* and, thereby, Zen. As explained by the samurai who became a Buddhist monk, Shiba Yoshimasa (1349-1410), Samurai should "behave in a manner considerate not only of their own honor, of course, but also of the honor of their descendants. They should not bring on eternal disgrace by solicitude for their limited lives." (Cleary, 2008: 18; cf. Pinguet, 1993). In clarification, Yoshimasa continued,

> That being said, nevertheless to regard your one and only life as like dust or ashes and die when you shouldn't is to acquire a worthless reputation. A genuine motive would be, for example, to give up your life for the sake of the sole sovereign ... [action in accordance with *Bushidō*] would convey an exalted name to children and descendants. Something like a strategy of the moment, whether good or bad, cannot raise the family reputation much. (Cleary, 2008: 18).

As expressed in the virtues of *Bushidō* the "honor" and nobility of a samurai are not isolated from family or descendants. Thus, opportunistic "strategy of the moment" comportment not only reveals a worldly, attached, monkey-mind, which may be seen as dishonorable according to *Bushidō*.

No matter, then, how foreign it may appear at first to a Western-mind-set, "suicide in Japan is viewed as a potentially honorable, virtuous, and even beautiful act of self-sacrifice expressing one's duty to one's group." (Young, 2002: 14). In regard to evaluating the individual's action as it relates to a moral code applicable beyond the individual, it is as if the "values giving moral legitimacy to suicide run deeper than the act of suicide itself." (Young, 2002: 14). Yet, insofar as we may reduce "self-sacrifice" to a social level, the question remains regarding a more "cosmic" or "divine" level. In other words, it is usually the case that self-murder, i.e. suicide, is prohibited, just like other-murder on grounds such as karma.

As we noted above, commentaries on *seppuku* often characterize it "as an aid to enlightenment" (cf. Morillo, 2001: 248). On the one hand, then, we may simply ask: How is it possible that suicide could be characterized in terms of Japanese philosophy and religion as good? On the other hand, we will examine – what to my mind – may be one of the most "tragically"-beautiful articulations of a relation to karmic-logic possible. That is, to be willing to endure a longer sojourn in hell for the sake of *Bushidō* generally, and doing one's duty more specifically.

In regard to the former question, there are essentially three different approaches toward an answer. First, the approach we may call "setting things right," which is non-metaphysically-oriented:

> Among a savage tribe which has no marriage, adultery is not a sin, and only the jealousy of a lover protects a woman from abuse: so in a time which has no criminal court, murder is not a crime, and only the vigilant vengeance of the victim's people preserves social order. "What is the most beautiful thing on earth?" said Osiris to Horus. The reply was, "To avenge a parent's wrongs," – to which a Japanese would have added "and a master's." (Inazō, 1908: 116).

Second, the approach we may call the "permissible" approach, which is metaphysically-oriented. On the one hand,

> Although Buddhism is ostensibly the only one of the Japanese religious and philosophical traditions featuring an explicit prohibition of killing, this proscription was not considered applicable to soldier-monks in monastic armies envisioned as protectors of Buddhism, nor to samurai in their role as police and protectors of society and state. (Cleary, 2008: 6).

On the other hand,

There are, however, passages in the *Nikayas*
where the Buddha approves of the suicide of
bhikkus: but in these cases they were Arahants
[i.e. Arhats], and we are to suppose that such
beings who have mastered self, can do what
they please as regards the life and death of their
carcass. (Woodward, 1922: 8; cf. Becker, 1990;
cf. *Samyutta Nikaya* I, §121).

Thus, in both of these cases, murder – and even the self-
sacrificing murder of suicide – seems permissible. Further,
to put "permissible" in more metaphysical terms would be
to say something like, these individuals may be understood
as achieving "final nirvana" through suicide, and therefore
not "condemned" to re-incarnation due to suicide.

Finally, recall above we mentioned the notion of a
"revengeful ghost," which may be understood as related,
for example, to "hungry ghosts" from our discussion of re-
incarnation and karma. The idea there, of course, was that
re-incarnation may in several ways be characterized in
opposition to nirvana, for example, in the context of the
"Wheel of Birth and Re-Birth," nirvana may be described
as a kind of Buddha-birth or becoming Buddha. It is in this
context, then, that the following passage should be read:

Although it is unfitting for someone like me to
say this, in dying it is my hope not to become a
Buddha. Rather, my will is permeated with the
resolution to help manage the affairs of the
province, though I be reborn as a Nabeshima
samurai seven times. One needs neither vitality
nor talent. In a word, it is a matter of having
the will to shoulder the clan by oneself.
(Yamamoto, 2011: 146).

Clearly metaphysically-oriented, the hallmark of this
approach is the samurai's willingness to endure a longer
sojourn in hell for the sake of *Bushidō* generally, or duty
specifically – karma be what it may.

§16 *Poet-Warrior-Monks & the Artistry of Death*

In Western terms we may say that the Spirit of
Nature is omnipresent, and when individual hearts are
open to its influence, it becomes possible to speak of the

Holy Spirit and the Grace of God, insofar as the influence of the Spirit is consistent with Holiness (cf. Scalambrino, 2015a). In Eastern terms, then, the gracefulness of the Zen monks, the samurai, and the haiku poets may be understood as a kind of omni-*present* "holding-open" oneself to the influence of the Spirit of Nature. It would be as if the wind blowing through the trees may be the grace-full Holy Spirit/Spirit of Heaven; thus, the ancient Shintō animism speaks of "*kami*," i.e. "heaven," and we gain insight into the "wind of heaven." Just as the breeze gracefully cuts the cherry blossoms, so too the Way of the Samurai ("*Hana wa sakura ni, hito wa bushi*"), dying when it is time to die, is the Way of Heaven.

i. *Absolute Motion & Cut: Calligraphy & Death*

Recall "cut" (*kire*) here is a quadruple entendre in that it is sword cut, flower cut, poem cut, and *kami* cut. *Bushidō*, like its more modern counterpart *Budō*, involved not only the study of war (*bu*) but also the study of Japanese fine arts (*dō*, i.e. "the path"), such as *Shodō* (calligraphy), *Kadō* (the Way of Flowers/*ikebana*), *Sadō* (the Way of Tea/Japanese tea ceremony), poetry (*Waka*), etiquette and music (e.g. *Shōmyō*), and philosophy. For example, in regard to calligraphy:

> For is not the ability to make the stroke flow naturally, to let the brush move freely across a thin piece of paper, also a superior struggle of the most testing kind? The spontaneous stroke of the brush is reminiscent of the quick free thrust of the sword or the freedom of the arrow fired effortlessly. Wherever there is distress, worry or uneasiness, there can be no perfect freedom or swiftness of action. (Random, 1978: 98).

What is more, in regard to the art of flower arranging:

> Such art changes with the season and reveals its beauty only for the few days after the flowers and branches have been cut. It is by its very nature, something temporary and improvised. The essential beauty lies precisely in its being transitory and timely. It is beauty which

appears out of the impermanency of time itself. (Nishitani, 1995: 23).

The characterization in terms of temporariness and improvisation helps point directly to the "emptiness" of constant practice at "cutting-off" the karmic spinning mind (cf. Suzuki, 2011). Insofar as this points to the revelation of the eternal within the temporary, then this "cut" may be helped by the habit-force exemplified by the "spirit of repetition" and a kind of harmonic alignment with absolute motion – *kami* and karmic momentariness.

> Recalling the above discussion in the ninja section,
> In all the martial arts, in all the performing arts and still more in all the forms of human behavior, a man's postures or moves are based on the movements of [the invisible emptiness of] his mind… [In this style of] swordsmanship a swordsman reads his opponent's mind through his postures or moves…
> What mind can penetrate his opponent's mind? It is a mind that has been trained and cultivated to the point of detachment with perfect freedom. It is as clear as a mirror that can reflect the motions within his opponent's mind… when one stands face to face with his opponents, his mind must not be revealed in the form of moves. Instead his mind should reflect his opponent's mind like water reflecting the moon. (Sugawara, 1988: 95-7).

The samurai ability – which is also the ability of the Zen monk and haiku poet – to find Zen, then, cuts-off the karmic spinning mind *and* the situational-directedness of the empty freedom apperceptively perceives the opponents apperception, a process resembling the "pure conversations" of Daoist and Buddhist monks.

In a way that reminds of Van Gogh's philosophy of painting, one must work with the material and the material nature of what is operative in a situation. There is, of course, form, and the material is to-be-formed with the skill of the practitioner; however, this is "improvisation" insofar as the operative (temporary) configurations involved require the form to be "evanescent."

The three shouts are divided thus: before, during, and after. *Shout according to the situation.* The voice is a thing of life... The voice shows energy... In single combat, we make *as if to cut* and shout "Ei!" at the same time to disturb the enemy, then in the wake of our shout we cut with the long sword. We shout after we have cut down the enemy – this is to announce victory. This is called *sen go no koe* (before and after voice). We do not shout simultaneously with flourishing the long sword. We shout during the fight to get into rhythm. Research this deeply [emphases added]. (Miyamoto, 2011: 41-42).

To "get into rhythm" here, then, reminds of the practitioner's ability to skillfully remain in harmony with an (omni-*present*) evanescent form.

This is the art of "practicing death." As if channeling the Dharmakāya light of death or harmonically-synching oneself with the absolute divine motion (*kami*), the power of habit allows one to endure being the vessel for such absolute motion. For example, in regard to samurai training,

at the sound of a sharp command, a warrior squatting in the middle of a mat (often blindfolded) would rise, his sword being instantly unsheathed in a single fluid, and circular motion as he slashed at the four or more targets set on poles which had been placed at the borders of the mat. Without any interruption of the initial sweeping motion, he would return his sword to its sheath and resume his squatting position. The time it took him to accomplish the entire sequence was duly computed and reduced to a flashing moment by rigorous, continuous training. (Ratti and Westbrook, 1973: 279).

A more strictly Zen articulation comes from *Zen and the Martial Arts*,

When you think of showing off your skill or defeating an opponent, your self-consciousness

will interfere with the performance... There
must be the absence of the feeling that you are
doing it... Now you have the key to the ancient
Zen riddle, "When you seek it, you cannot find
it." (Hyams, 1979: 85).

Finally, as Suzuki put it, to endure being the vessel of
absolute motion is to keep your "beginner's mind."

The seed has no idea of being some particular
plant, but it has its own form and is in perfect
harmony with the ground, with its
surroundings. As it grows, in the course of time
it expresses its nature. Nothing exists without
form and color. Whatever it is, it has some form
and color, and that form and color are in perfect
harmony with other beings. And there is no
trouble. That is what we mean by naturalness.
(Suzuki, 2011: 97).

Of course, human freedom, or freedom of will, makes the
situatedness for humans different from stones and plants.
"For a plant or stone to be natural is no problem. But for
us there is some problem... To be natural is something
which we must work on. When what you do just comes out
from nothingness, you have quite a new feeling." (Suzuki,
2011: 97). To stay in harmony with the rhythm of this
nothingness is to live in the light of death.

In regard to this "nothingness" (cf. Scalambrino,
2011), Suzuki explained,

There is something, but that something is
something which is always prepared for taking
some particular form, and it has some rules, or
theory, or truth in its activity. This is called
Buddha nature, or Buddha himself. When this
existence is personified we call it Buddha; when
we understand it as the ultimate truth we call
it Dharma; and when we accept the truth and
act as a part of the Buddha, or according to the
theory, we call ourselves Sangha. But even
though there are three Buddha forms, it is one
existence which has no form or color, and it is
always ready to take form and color. (Suzuki,
2011: 107).

According to Suzuki, then, the Three Jewels of Buddhism may be invoked to characterize the absoluteness of motion, referred to before as the wind of heaven, Rupakāya and Dharmakāya. And, the cut may be understood as a "violent reassertion of form." As such, the reassertion of *form* refers to harmonizing the situation with *Bushidō*.

ii. *The Doctrine of Dying Like a Madman*

Keeping in mind, then, that samurai were trained in the fine arts such as poetry and calligraphy, many samurai, especially as a ritualized component of *seppuku*, constructed a final poem, prior to death, and these poems have come to be called "Death Poems." The Introduction to *Japanese Death Poems: Written by Zen Monks and Haiku Poets on the Verge of Death* invokes the *Hagakure* discussing the proper manner of a knight in regard to death, noting, "the key feature in the way of the samurai is his ability to die. The samurai … ought to 'die like a madman.'" (Hoffman, 1986: 41).

According to Saito Totsudo (1797-1865) in regard to the relation between "the manner of a knight" and the "warrior spirit,"

> Once the manner of a knight is proper, it is essential to cultivate the warrior spirit. While maintaining the manner of a knight is for the purpose of cultivating the warrior spirit, insofar as manner is a matter of external appearance, however awesome it may be, it cannot be relied upon on a deep level. When the spirit fills your being like blazing fire… that is rather more reliable.
>
> Thus, it is when the warrior spirit is effective that the manner of the knight is truly firm. Even if your physical strength is above ordinary, if your spirit flinches you can't face opponents effectively. However skillful you may be in martial arts, if your spirit flinches you can't use them against opponents. So, it is when filled with spirit that intelligence and courage are effective. (Cleary, 2008: 235; cf. Scalambrino, 2015a).

"The same spirit of uncompromising fanaticism that appears in the life histories and death poems of samurai near the end of the Edo period can be felt among the monarchists and nationalists of the late nineteenth- and early-twentieth centuries. (Hoffman, 1986: 42). Moreover, in the contemporary period the Japanese government's "propaganda machine" "produced books, including children's books and textbooks, containing stories about warriors dying a martyr's death and quoting death poems of bravery and resignation to fate." (Ibid).

It should not be too surprising, then, to discover that the word "*kaze*" means "wind," such that "Kamikaze" literally means "the wind of heaven" or "the wind of the gods." And, the kamikaze suicide manual prescribes "shouting." For example, "Remember when diving into the enemy to shout at the top of your lungs: '*Hissatsu!*' [Sink without fail!]. At that moment, all the cherry blossoms at Yasukuni shrine in Tokyo will smile brightly at you." (Axell and Kase, 2002: 82).

V.
Zen Poets: From Kōans to Haiku

"This is not a place we remain for long. The death-dealing
demon of impermanence comes in an instant, without
discriminating between noble and base, old and young."
~Linji Yixuan, *The Record of Linji*.
(2008: 9).

§17 *What is a Kōan?*

Though much may be said about kōans and
traditions which invoke kōans, we will answer the question
"What is a kōan?" in five ways. First, a general articulation
of what a kōan is. Second, we will discuss the intellectual
approach to kōans; third, the experiential approach.
Fourth, we will briefly consider how kōans may be
understood as "existential karma puzzles." Finally, we will
look at a bouquet of kōans.

Kōans are often characterized as "cases," "puzzles,"
or "epigrams." A commonality of characterizing kōans in
these ways, then, emphasizes their elusive nature and
tendency to produce spontaneous insight, as if by surprise.
Thus, there is an "intellectual approach" to the study of
kōans. Through the intellectual approach student and
teacher engage in a discussion of Buddhist ideas and
teachings expressed in kōans. In this way, the intellectual
approach tends toward a more dichotomous
understanding of themes and ideas expressed through
kōans. That is, it makes sense within the context of the
intellectual approach to say that a student's interpretation
is "right" or "wrong." For example, we will see this
dramatized in the fourth of the kōans to follow.

Beyond the intellectual approach we may speak of
an "experiential approach" to the study of kōans.
Traditionally a master may ask a student to meditate with
a kōan in mind. This is often characterized in terms of a
student's "embodying" the kōan, rather than trying to

"solve" it. For, "the point of kōan practice is to attain a nonrational, direct insight beyond the boundaries of language and conceptual thought" (Hori, 2003: 4). After meditating with the kōan, the student would be expected to express an understanding of the kōan, and this understanding should be "direct and dynamic," not a "high-flown intellectual" interpretation. This experiential approach is called "*Dokusan.*"

An even more "existential" approach to kōans, then, calls for us to consider our momentary situational experiences as so many kōans. Yet, to be clear, this may be understood in multiple ways. On the one hand, we could understand our current existential situation as directly related to the theme of some kōan. In this way, it would be like saying: "Hey! This situation reminds me of the 'Muddy Road' kōan." On the other hand, we could understand our current existential situation in terms of so many variables upon which we may find ourselves dwelling or preoccupied. In this way, our relation to the variables may remind us of some kōan or aspect of a kōan such that we may change our relation to the variable(s) through our recollection of a kōan-study-gained insight. Further, we could understand our current existential situation as resulting from karma, and, in this way, we may think of our existential situation as itself a kōan. Thus, not only would our kōan-study-gained insights perhaps help us navigate our various existential situations, but also we may relate to our various existential situations as so many karmically-constructed kōans.

The following six (6) kōans have been hand-picked for you from the Zen Master, and founder of the Sōtō School of Zen, Dōgen's (Dōgen Zenji) collection of kōans and *Zen Flesh Zen Bones: A Collection of Zen and Pre-Zen Writings.*

i. "*A Cup of Tea*"
"Nan-In, a Japanese master during the Meiji era (1862-1912), received a university professor who came to inquire about Zen. Nan-In served tea. He poured his visitor's cup full, and then kept on pouring.

The professor watched the overflow until he no longer could restrain himself. 'It is overfull. No more will go in!'

'Like this cup,' Nan-In said, 'you are full of your own opinions and speculations. How can I show you Zen unless you first empty your cup?'" (Reps and Senzaki, 1998: 19).

ii. *"Muddy Road"*

Three monks were traveling together down a muddy road, while the rain was still pouring. As they turned a corner they encountered a "lovely girl in a silk kimono and sash, unable to cross the intersection."

The monks lifted her off the ground and carried her across the muddy intersection.

Later that evening the first monk said, "We monks don't go near females." Suggesting perhaps the monks should not have lifted her above the mud.

Resonating with this idea, the second monk noted, "especially not young and lovely females." Echoing and emphasizing the suggestion that perhaps the monks should not have lifted her above the mud.

Suddenly the third monk spoke, "I left the girl there ... Are you still carrying her?" (cf. Reps and Senzaki, 1998: 33).

iii. *"Real Prosperity"*

"A rich man asked Sengai to write something for the continued prosperity of his family so that it might be treasured from generation to generation.

Sengai obtained a large sheet of paper and wrote: 'Father dies, son dies, grandson dies.'

The rich man became angry. 'I asked you to write something for the happiness of my family! Why do you make such a joke as this?'

'No joke is intended,' explained Sengai. 'If before you yourself die your son should die, this would grieve you greatly. If your grandson should pass away before your son, both of you would be broken-hearted. If your family, generation after generation, passes away in the order I have named, it will be the natural course of life. I call this real prosperity.'" (cf. Reps and Senzaki, 1998: 89).

iv. *"Not the Wind, Not the Flag"*
"Two monks were arguing about a flag. One said: 'The flag is moving.'

The other said: 'The wind is moving.'

The sixth patriarch happened to be passing by.
He told them: 'Not the wind, not the flag; mind is moving.'"
(cf. Reps and Senzaki, 1998: 143-4).

v. *"Stop Illusory Thinking"*
"Changsha was once asked by Emperor's Secretary Du,
'When you chop an earthworm into two pieces, both pieces keep moving. I wonder, in which piece is the buddha nature?'
Changsha said, 'Don't have illusory thoughts.'
Du said, 'How are we to understand that they are both moving?'
Changsha said, 'Understand that air and fire are not yet scattered.' Du said nothing.
Changsha called Du, and Du responded 'Yes?'
Changsha said, 'Isn't this your true self?'
Du said, 'Apart from my answering, is there another true self?'
Changsha said, 'I can't call you Emperor.'
Du said, 'If so, would my not answering also be my true self?'
Changsha said, 'It's not a matter of answering me or not.
But since the beginningless *kalpa* [(aeon)], the question to answer or not has been the root of birth and death' Then he recited a verse:

> Students of the Way don't know the truth.
> They only know their past consciousness.
> This is the basis of birth and death.
> The deluded call it the original self."

(Dōgen, 2005: 28).
The following, then, is considered the kōan's "Capping Verse."
"Bright day, blue sky –
> in a dream he tries to explain his dream.
See! The myriad forms arising and vanishing,
> all abiding in their own dharma place,
> constantly reveal the buddha nature." (Ibid.).

vi. *"Cut a Fine Piece"*

"Once Zen master Panshan went to the marketplace and overheard a customer speaking to the butcher. The customer said to the butcher, 'Cut a fine piece for me.'

The butcher threw down his knife, folded his hands, and said, 'Sir, is there any piece that is not fine?'

Upon hearing these words, Panshan had an awakening." (Dōgen, 2005: 29).

Coda: Capping Phrases

A brief word about Zen "Capping Phrases" is called for, insofar as it helps connect the practice of writing kōans to the practice of writing haiku. Recall that the "two schools of Zen," i.e. Rinzai and Sōtō, are often differentiated from one another in terms of the kōan practice; it is despite the fact that Dōgen is largely credited with transmitting the practice from China to Japan, it is the school he founded, i.e. the Sōtō School, which is characterized as having cut off kōan practice. Thus,

> Rinzai monasteries in Japan vary in the way they conduct kōan practice, but in the Myōshin-ji-Daitoku-ji branch, when a monk has passed a kōan the Zen teacher will instruct him to bring a "capping phrase," called *jakugo* or *agyo*. The monk selects a verse or phrase that expresses the insight he has had while meditating on the kōan. He searches for this capping phrase in one of the several Zen phrase books that have been especially compiled for this purpose. (Hori, 2003: 3-4).

In this way, becoming adept with "capping phrases" means obtaining direct insight through kōan study *and* identifying the insight with one of the many traditional Zen capping phrases.

There are higher levels to be attained in regard to kōan study and *jakugo*.

> If the monk continues into advanced stages of the Rinzai Zen kōan curriculum, he will receive further literary assignments: the writing of explanations in Japanese, called *kakiwake*,

91

and the composition of Chinese-style poetry, called *nenro*. Such literary study is not merely an incidental part of kōan training. (Hori, 2003: 4).

The literary assignments, then, assigned to monks at "advanced stages" amount to the construction of kōan "explanations," poems, and capping phrases. Further, because these capping phrases range from four (4) to twenty-one (21) or more characters in length, many Zen capping phrases may be constructed as poems, and the construction itself likened to the construction of haiku.

The following examples of capping phrases come from *Zen Sand: The book of capping phrases for Kōan practice*:

"If you want to obtain what's right before your eyes, don't take the opposite as real." (Hori, 2003: 328).

"Beautiful snow! Flake after flake, they fall in no other place." (Ibid: 329).

"We drunkenly see the ground of actuality as 'my world.'" (Ibid: 337).

"The wind stops, but the flowers still fall; A bird sings and the mountain is quieter still." (Ibid: 381).

"I've heard it said sorrow is hard to banish, But these words are not true." (Ibid: 383).

"Flowers bloom to many winds and rains, A person's life is filled with partings." (Hori, 2003: 384).

"Every day is a good day. When the wind blows, the tree nods." (Ibid: 429).

"There is no shame more shameful than having many desires, There is no joy more joyous than non-seeking." (Ibid: 431).

"This thing, that thing, are all originally dharmas;
This thought, that thought, are nothing other than mind."
(Ibid: 437).

"Cage him and he will not stay put,
Call and he will not turn his head." (Ibid: 447).

"Everything is arrayed before one's very eyes,
All thought is cut off in the realm beyond measure."
(Ibid: 474).

"On the branches without buds, flowers bloom;
On the tree without shadow, the phoenix dances."
(Ibid: 475).

"See for yourself that on the path of life and death,
The live person is completely inside the dead person."
(Ibid: 533).

"The garden trees are unaware
the people have gone away.
When spring comes,
they send forth flowers as always." (Ibid: 555).

"It is like the stone – unaware of the flawless perfection of
the jewel that it possesses within itself.
It resembles the earth – unaware of the solitary grandeur
of the mountain that it supports." (Ibid: 618).

§18 *What is a Haiku Poem?*
The word "Haiku" comes from "Hokku" meaning the starting verse of a long and sing-song "Renga" poem. Structural criteria are not strictly maintained when translating from Japanese to English, though traditionally haiku are structured by three lines with 5-7-5 syllables, respectively. Haiku are characterized by "overcondensation" and "surprise." In regard to overcondensation, it is as if through the use of traditionally recognized references haiku concisely evoke visions or recollections with intricate depth. For example, the

93

changing seasons, plants, and animals are specifically and traditionally associated with moods and ideas.

Haiku may be said to adhere to a trinity of conventions: (1) describing a single event, (2) the time being the present, and (3) with reference to nature. That is, the process of composing a haiku may be characterized as perceiving the existential situation of a moment and "translating" it into language. Importantly, readers of haiku are to pause after each line to allow the meaning of each line of the poem to emerge prior to reading the next line. This practice allows for the full effect of the "surprise" or "cutting" which haiku perform. That is to say, each of the first two lines may have separate meanings, and the juxtaposition of these meanings may contribute further to the overall meaning. The meaning which emerges from the third line, then, punctuates the meaning carried to its threshold, changing or coloring the meaning of the poem, which had thus far emerged, in a surprising way.

On the one hand, haiku poets use this traditional form, including the overcondensation beyond syllabic structure, to "translate" a moment's experience into language. On the other hand, the "cutting" or surprise component of haiku poems resonates well with the "capping phrase" (*Jakugo*) from the kōan tradition. Just as kōans were characterized as "puzzles," or "epigrams," so too Zen inspired haiku may be understood intellectually or experientially. Thus, a haiku may produce spontaneous insight, as if by surprise, through the intellectual process of understanding its expression of Buddhist themes or through the experiential process of a reader "embodying" the poem, recollecting the poet's recollection, as if to induce a repetition of the moment's enlightenment.

Viewing each of the moments in the light of death allows us to appreciate the Zen-inspired haiku poet's awareness of impermanence (*anicca*), and non-substantiality (*anattā*). It is often said that the greatest of the Japanese haiku poets are Bashō, Buson, and Issa. Regarding these three, Bashō is of such importance that a separate section of the chapter is devoted to him. Before reading the following celebrated haiku, it will be helpful to consider the following themed-lists of words, if we are to appreciate the overcondensation involved.

In regard to the Spring Season, the moods expressed include: Anticipation; Awe; Being loved; Companionship; Desire; Dreams; Hope; Infidelity; Jealousy; Joy; Passion; Pleasure; New life; Seduction. The animal words used include: Bees; Beetles; Birds; Caterpillars; Cats; Cuckoos; Fireflies; Frogs; Hummingbirds; Storks; Tadpoles; Ticks. Finally, the plant words used to invoke Spring and its moods include: Apple trees; Blossoms; Buds; Cherry trees; Daffodils; Daisies; Dandelions; Flowers; Pansies; Plums; Roses; Strawberries; Tulips; Lilac.

In regard to Summer, the moods expressed include: After loving; Anger; Being lazy; Dancing; Desire to travel; Dread of Autumn; Enjoyment; Fickleness; Kissing; Laughter; Memories; Openness; Panic; Pride; Relief. The animal words used include: Ants; Bats; Butterflies; Cicadas; Cuckoos; Flies; Gnats; Geese; Grasshoppers; Hornets; Lady bugs; Mosquitos; Peacocks; Snakes; Wrens. Finally, the plant words used to invoke the Summer Season and its accompanying moods include: Apricots; Azaleas; Bananas; Bamboo; Blackberries; Cacti; Carrots; Melons; Mint; Morning-glories; Peaches; Peppers; Water lilies; Weeds.

In regard to Autumn, the moods expressed include: Abandonment; Aging; Arguments; Decay; Deception; Emptiness; Endings; Fears; Grief; Jealousy; Loneliness; Longing; Loss; Regrets; Rest; Sadness; Worries. The animal words used include: Cicadas; Deer; Owls; Salmon; Scorpions; Squirrels; Turkeys; Vultures. Finally, the plant words used to invoke the Autumn Season and its accompanying moods include: Acorns; Buckeyes; Chestnuts; Chrysanthemums; Cottonwoods; Corn; Driftwood; Mushrooms; Onions; Pumpkins; Straw; Vines; Willows.

In regard to Winter, the moods expressed include: Boredom; Calmness; Depression; Discipline; Estrangement; Helplessness; Isolation; Madness; Pain; Peacefulness; Release; Remembering; Restlessness; Solitude; Quietude. The animal words used include: Bears; Blackbirds; Doves; Eagles; Fish; Geese; Horses; Monkeys;

Mice; Owls. Finally, the plant words used to invoke the Winter Season and its accompanying moods include: Branches without blossoms; Evergreens; Fir; Pine; Roots; Snow covered plants; Tulip stems; Withered leaves.[1]

In regard to other traditional themes: the Japanese cuckoo is associated with dusk and wisdom (cf. Henderson, 1958: 6). Similarly, just as "morning-glories bring up thoughts of quickly fading beauty ... and plum blossoms the promise of perfect beauty to be attained by the later cherry blossom," so too cherry blossoms bring to mind thoughts of impermanence and poppies refer to sleep and death (cf. Henderson, 1958: 6; cf. Blyth, 1973a&b; cf. Higginson, 1996).

i. *Onitsura (1661-1738)*

"The autumn wind
blowing across
    peoples faces"

"A trout leaps;
clouds are moving
    in the bed of the stream."

"No place
to throw out the bathwater –
sound of insects"[2]

---

[1] I consider these lists "common property" in that these lists may be compiled from simply reading traditional haiku extensively, and, moreover, I no longer remember all the sources from which some of these terms may have been found.

[2] Bowers, 1996: 38-40.

ii. *Buson (1716-1784)*

"He's on the porch,
to escape the wife and kids –
how hot it is!"

"Before the white chrysanthemum
the scissors hesitate
a moment."

My arm for a pillow,
I really like myself
under the hazy moon.[3]

iii. *Issa (1763-1828)*

"New Year's Day –
everything is in blossom!
I feel about average."

"Goes out,
comes back –
the love life of a cat."

"A cuckoo sings
to me, to the mountain
to me, to the mountain."

"Don't cry, wild geese,
it's the same everywhere –
this floating world."[4]

---

[3] Hass, 1994: 79-127.
[4] Saito and Nelson, 2006: 257-266.

§19 *Bashō as Archetype of the Haiku Poet*

In 1644 Matsuo Bashō was born into a samurai family, and by "1679, he had become a lay Zen monk ... and took up residence in a hut [by a river] on the outskirts of the city. [His poetry within this period showed] an increasingly dark tone, some bordering on desolation" (Barnhill, 2004: 11). Moreover, according to another translator, Bashō became "the most famous Japanese writer of all time," since the haiku poetry of his contemporaries lacked "the ability to capture both the momentary and the eternal in a small poem" (Reichhold, 2008: 7-9). We also hear of Bashō's style that he would often leave "a 'hermeneutical space,' a gap in the meaning of the poem that invites the reader in to complete the poem in her own experience" (Barnhill, 2004: 14). Essentially Bashō was a wandering poet who journaled his travels with poems commemorating events. Often he would bring joy to villages along the way, and we hear the following from his famous *The Narrow Road to the Deep North*: "It was indeed a great pleasure for me to be of such help during my wandering journey" (Bashō, 1966: 123).

i. *Mōnō Nō Aware*

As an aesthetic ideal, *mōnō nō aware* (pronounced "moh-noh noh ah-wah-ray") suggests a sensitivity or awareness, e.g. regarding the skandhas, that responds to the presence of objects, living beings, or the affective states of living beings. Because the content of life is impermanent, everything we love in "the world" will eventually die. Like the *memento mori* of the Buddhist "Five Remembrances" it is clear that this body must eventually die. Affected, then, by the impermanence and temporariness of things and life events, the human response is, of course, a kind of *pathos* or feeling, and most often some kind of "melancholic appreciation" or "sorrow." When kōans, capping verses, and haiku are able to lyrically capture the natural human affectivity while simultaneously communicating an enlightened unattachment to the transience of the situation, then they perform a kind of "pure conversation" with their readers.

As one commentator, regarding "evanescence and form" and "the order of here-and-now" explained,

> The lyrical thrust of Japanese aesthetics points us to a breakdown of the barriers between the self and its surroundings, between the inner and the outer. And yet, this emotionalism is also strangely and strictly formal and predictable. No doubt, this predisposition to become one with the moment... that is presupposed in the lyrical apprehension of one's context is neither chaotic nor nihilistic since even a spontaneous (*jihatsu*) response to one's context must stay within the parameters of form. (Inouye, 2008: 84).

Notice the analogy, then, the relation between the situated-momentary content and art-*form* through which it is being expressed mirror the relation between the karmically-situated-person and the path of enlightenment. Having just mentioned this in terms of a "pure conversation" performed by haiku, we will consider *Kadō* (the Way of Flowers/*ikebana*) as it also includes the notion of cut.

Though the Japanese "Way of Flowers," is called *Kadō*, the art of arranging the flowers is called *ikebana*, which translates as "to keep flowers alive" (Hepburn, 1894: 195). Thus, it is as if the cut and the situated-momentary arrangement of the flowers "keep them alive." As Nishitani explained *ikebana*,

> Death in which life has been severed, or nothingness (*mu*) in which the possibilities of existence have been cut off – this is not a mere natural death. The natural death of flowers lies in withering and decaying, and arranged flowers must be thrown out before they wither. The death of flowers that have been severed while living transcends the life of nature, transcends the constructs of time, and signifies a movement into new life as a moment. This nothingness is the attainment of new possibilities of existence as a temporary manifestation of eternity within time. (1995: 25).

Notice, the language of "temporary manifestation of eternity within time" pertains specifically to the discussion of haiku and Zen, and generally to *mōnō nō aware*.

ii. *Bashō (1644-1694)*

#501 – "No bell ringing
what does the village do?
spring evening."

> #11 – "Among blossoms
> grieving that I can't even open
> my poem bag."

> #152 – "At the ancient pond
> a frog plunges into
> the sound of water."

> #445 – "Morning glories
> ignoring the revelers
> in full bloom."

> #1009 – "Evening orchid –
> the white of its flower
> hidden in its scent."

> #942 – "Did it sing
> till it became all voice?
> Cicada-shell!"

#394 – "On Buddha's birthday
a spotted fawn is born –
just like that."

> #254 – "Reluctantly
> the bee emerges from deep within
> the peony

#164 – "Wake up! Wake up!
let's be friends,
sleeping butterfly."

#137 – "Folly in darkness
grasping a thorn
instead of a firefly."

#911 – "A spring night
and with dawn on the cherries,
it has ended."

#661 – "Nothing in the cry of cicadas
suggests
they are about to die."

#279 – "How I long to see
among dawn flowers
the face of God."

#179 – cuckoo
now as for haiku masters
none are in this world

#709 – "Year after year
the cherry tree nourished
by fallen blossoms."

#37 – "In my humble view
the netherworld must be like this –
autumn evening."[5]

---

[5] All numbers refer to: *Bashō: The Complete Haiku.* Jane Reichhold, translator.

§20 *What is a Death Poem?*

The Japanese word for "Death Poem" is *Jisei*. It means: "Leaving the world; poetry composed by a person about to die" (Hepburn, 1894: 226). They have been compared to writing on gravestones.

> Historically, most death poems have been in tanka form, those composed by the court nobility refined and delicate, and those by warriors more "masculine" ... Later, Chinese death poems were written by Buddhist monks and priests, by scholars of Chinese literature, and to a fair extent by samurai. Death poems in haiku form, appearing first in the sixteenth century, have been written by Japanese from all levels of society. (Hoffman, 1986: 43).

The following *jisei* were written in haiku form, and illustrate, according to the Zen monks and samurai discussed above, a kind of resolute calmness in greeting death which comes from living in the light of death.

i. *Yoshitoshi (d. 1892)*

> "Holding back the night
> with its increasing brilliance
> the summer moon."[6]

ii. *Gozan (d. 1733)*

> "The snow of yesterday
> that fell like cherry petals
> is water once again."[7]

iii. *Hokushi (d. 1718)*

> "I write, erase, rewrite,
> erase again, and then
> a poppy blooms."[8]

---

[6] *One Hundred Aspects of the Moon*, p. 7.
[7] *Japanese Death Poems*, pp. 178-179.
[8] *Japanese Death Poems*, p. 190.

iv. *Joseki (d. 1779)*

"This must be,
my birthday there
in paradise."[9]

v. *Kangyu (d. 1861)*

"It is indeed like that –
and I had never noticed
dew on grass."[10]

vi. *Mabutsu (d. 1874)*

"Moon in a barrel:
you never know just when
the bottom will fall out."[11]

vii. *Shutei (d. 1858)*

"From on a summer day
all I leave behind is water
that has washed my brush."[12]
(A reference to the brush used to write this poem.)

viii. *Bokusui (d. 1914)*

"A parting word?
The melting snow
is odorless."[13]

---

[9] *Japanese Death Poems*, pp. 207-208.
[10] *Japanese Death Poems*, pp. 213-214.
[11] *Japanese Death Poems*, p. 239.
[12] *Japanese Death Poems*, p. 307.
[13] *Japanese Death Poems*, p. 146.

Bibliography

Adolphson, Mikael S. (2007). *The Teeth and Claws of the Buddha: Monastic Warriors and* Sōhei *in Japanese History*. Honolulu, HI: The University Press of Hawaii.

Arch, J., and M. Craske. (2006). Mechanisms of mindfulness: Emotion regulation following a focused breathing induction. *Behavior Research and Therapy* 44, 1849-1858.

Aristotle. (2009). *Nicomachean Ethics*. R. Crisp (Trans.). Cambridge: Cambridge University Press.

Axell, Albert, and Hideaki Kase. (2002). *Kamikaze: Japan's Suicide Gods*. London: Longman Pearson.

Barnes, V.A., H.C. Davis, J.B. Murzynowski, and F.A. Treiber. (2004). Impact of meditation on resting and ambulatory blood pressure and heart rate in youth. *Psychosomatic Medicine* 66, 909-914.

Barnhill, D.L. (2004). Introduction: The Haiku of Poetry of Matsuo Bashō. *Bashō's Haiku: Selected Poems of Matsuo Bashō*. Albany, NY: SUNY Press.

Bashō, Matsuo. (1966). *The Narrow Road to the Deep North and Other Travel Sketches*. N. Yuasa, (Trans.). London: Penguin Books.

Becker, Carl B. (1990). Buddhist Views of Suicide and Euthanasia. *Philosophy East and West* 40(4): 543-555.

Beddoe, A., and S. Murphy. (2004). Does mindfulness decrease stress and foster empathy among nursing students? *The Journal of Nursing Education* 43, 305-312.

Blomberg, Catharina. (2000). *The Heart of the Warrior: Origins and Religious Background of the Samurai System in Feudal Japan*. Tokyo, Japan: Japan Library.

Bloom, Mia. (2005). *Dying to Kill: The Allure of Suicide Terror*. New York, NY: Columbia University Press.

Blyth, R.H. (Ed. and Trans.). (1973a). *A History of Haiku, Vol. 1: From the Beginnings up to Issa.* Tokyo, Japan: The Hokuseido Press.

_____. (1973b). *A History of Haiku, Vol. 2: From Issa up to the Present.* Tokyo, Japan: The Hokuseido Press.

Boorstein, S. (2002). *Pay Attention, for Goodness' Sake: Practicing the perfections of the heart – the Buddhist path of kindness.* New York, NY: Ballantine Books.

Cleary, Thomas. (1999). Introduction. In *Code of the Samurai.* T.E. Cleary (Ed. and Trans.). Tokyo, Japan: Tuttle Publishing.

_____. (Ed. and Trans.). (2008). *Training the Samurai Mind: A Bushido Sourcebook.* Boston, MA: Shambhala.

Confucius. (1893). *The Doctrine of the Mean.* In J. Legge (Ed. & Trans.). *The Chinese Classics.* Oxford, UK: Clarendon Press.

Dharmasiri, Gunapala. (1989). *The Fundamentals of Buddhist Ethics.* Antioch, CA: Golden Leaves Publishing.

Dōgen. Eihei. (1997). *Bendōwa ["The Wholehearted Way"] with Commentary by Kōsho U. Roshi.* O. Shohaku and Taigen D. Leighton. (Trans.). Boston, MA: Tuttle Publishing.

_____. (2007). *Shōbōgenzō: The Treasure House of the Eye of the True Teaching.* H. Nearman (Trans.). Mount Shasta, CA: Shast Abbey Press.

_____. (2005). *The True Dharma Eye: Zen Master Dōgen's Three Hundred Kōans.* K. Tanahashi and J.D. Loori (Trans.). Boston, MA: Shambhala.

Dumoulin, Heinrich. (1988). *Zen Buddhism: A History, India and China.* New York, NY: Macmillan Publishing Co.

Eitel, Ernest J. (1904). *Hand-Book of Chinese Buddhism Being A Sanskrit-Chinese Dictionary with Vocabularies of Buddhist Terms.* Tokyo, Japan: Sanshusha

Eliade, Mircea. (1964). *Shamanism: Archaic Techniques of Ecstasy.* W.R. Trask (Trans.). Princeton, NJ: Princeton University Press.

Evans-Wentz, Walter Y. (1960). Introduction. In *The Tibetan Book of the Dead.* W.Y. Evans-Wentz (Trans.). (pp. 1-84). Oxford, UK: Oxford University Press.

Evola, Julius. (1996). *The Doctrine of Awakening: The Attainment of Self-Mastery According to the Earliest Buddhist Texts.* H.E. Musson (Trans.). Rochester, VT: Inner Traditions International.

Fischer, Roland. (1971). A Cartography of the Ecstatic and Meditative States. *Science,* New Series 174 (4012): 897-904.

Fremantle, Francesca. (2001). *Luminous Emptiness: Understanding the Tibetan Book of the Dead.* Boston, MA: Shambhala.

Fuller, Paul. (2005). *The Notion of Ditthi in Theravāda Buddhism: The Point of View.* London: Routledge.

Goddard, Dwight C. (Ed.). (1932). *A Buddhist Bible: The Favorite Scriptures of the Zen Sect.* Thetford, VT: Beacon Press.

Goomaraswamy, Amanda. (1969). *Buddha and the Gospel of Buddhism.* New Hyde Park, NY: University Books.

Graham, Archie. (2008). Living with Death: Kierkegaard and the Samurai. In J. Giles (Ed.). *Kierkegaard and Japanese Thought.* (pp. 141-158). New York: Palgrave.

Hajime, Nakamura. (1967a). Consciousness of the Individual and the Universal Among the Japanese. In C.A. Moore (Ed.). *The Japanese Mind: Essentials of Japanese Philosophy and Culture.* (pp. 179-200). Honolulu, HI: The University Press of Hawaii.

_____. (1967b). Basic Features of the Legal, Political, and Economic Thought of Japan. In C.A. Moore (Ed.). *The Japanese Mind: Essentials of Japanese Philosophy and Culture.* (pp. 143-163). Honolulu, HI: The University Press of Hawaii.

Hanh, Thich Nhat. (2009). *Answers from the Heart*. Berkeley, CA: Parallax Press.

Hass, Robert. (Ed. and Trans.). (1994). *The Essential Haiku: Versions of Bashō, Buson, and Issa*. Hopewell, NJ: The Ecco Press.

Hearn, Lafcadio. (1966). *Japan's Religions: Shinto and Buddhism*. New Hyde Par, NY: University Books, Inc.

Henderson, Harold G. (1958). *An Introduction to Haiku: An Anthology of Poems and Poets from Bashō to Shiki*. Garden City, NY: Doubleday Anchor Books.

Hepburn, J.C. (1894). *Japanese-English and English-Japanese Dictionary*. London: Trübner & Co.

Hideo, Kishimoto. (1967). Some Japanese Cultural Traits and eligions. In C.A. Moore (Ed.). *The Japanese Mind: Essentials of Japanese Philosophy and Culture.*(pp. 110-121). Honolulu, HI: The University Press of Hawaii.

Higginson, William J. (1996). *The Haiku Seasons: Poetry of the Natural World*. New York, NY: Kodansha International.

Hoffman, Yoel. (Ed.). (1986). *Japanese Death Poems: Written by Zen Monks and Haiku Poets on the Verge of Death*. Boston: Charles E. Tuttle Publishing Co.

Hori, Victor Sōgen. (2003). *Zen Sand: The book of capping phrases for Kōan practice*. Honolulu, HI: The University Press of Hawaii.

Hyams, Joe. (1979). *Zen and the Martial Arts*. New York, NY: Bantam.

Inazō, Nitobe. (1908). *Bushido – The Soul of Japan*. Tokyo, Japan: Teibi Publishing Company.

Inouye, Charles Shirō. (2008). *Evanescence and Form: An Introduction to Japanese Culture*. New York, NY: Palgrave Macmillan.

Johansson, R.E.A. (1970). *The Psychology of Nirvana: A comparative study of the natural goal of Buddhism and the aims of modern Western psychology.* New York, NY: Anchor Books.

Jung, Carl G. (1960). The Tibetan Book of the Dead: Psychological Commentary. R.F.C. Hull (Trans.). In *The Tibetan Book of the Dead.* W.Y. Evans-Wentz (Trans.). (pp. xxxv-lii). Oxford, UK: Oxford University Press.

Kalupahana, David J. (1975). *Causality: The Central Philosophy of Buddhism.* Honolulu, HI: The University Press of Hawaii.

King, Winston L. (1995). *Zen and the Way of the Sword: Arming the Samurai Psyche.* Oxford, UK: Oxford University Press.

Lee, Bruce and John Little. (2000). *Striking Thoughts: Bruce Lee's Wisdom for Daily Living.* Hong Kong: Tuttle Publishing.

Leighton, Taigen D. (2007). *Visions of Awakening Space and Time: Dōgen and the* Lotus Sutra. Oxford, UK: Oxford University Press.

Liezi. (1990). *The Book of Lieh-Tzu: A Classic of the Tao.* A.C. Graham (Trans.). Columbia University Press.

Lodrö, Geshe Gendün. (1992). *Walking Through Walls: A Presentation of Tibetan Meditation.* Ithaca, NY: Snow Lion.

Luk, Charles. (1970). Foreword. In C. Luk (Ed.). *Chán and Zen Teaching.* (pp. 9-18). Berkeley, CA: Shambhala.

Mason, J.W.T. (1967). *The Meaning of Shintō: The Primeval Foundation of Creative Spirit in Modern Japan.* Port Washington, NY: Kennikat Press.

Matics, Marion L. (1970). Guide to the Bodhicaryāvatāra. In M.L. Matics (Trans and Ed), *The Bodhicaryāvatāra of the Buddhist poet Śāntideva.* (pp. 11-140). London: Collier-Macmillan.

Bibliography

Matsunaga, Daigan and Alicia Matsunaga. (1974). *Foundation of Japanese Buddhism, Vol. I: The Aristocratic Age.* Los Angeles, CA: Buddhist Books International.

_____. (1976). *Foundation of Japanese Buddhism, Vol. II: The Mass Movement (Kamakura & Muromachi Periods).* Los Angeles, CA: Buddhist Books International.

Merriam-Webster.com 2017. http://www.merriam-webster.com. Accessed 02-20-2017.

Miyamoto, Musashi. (2011). *The Book of Five Rings.* In The Samurai Series. J.H. Ford and S. Conners (Eds.). El Paso, Tx: El Paso Norte Press.

Morillo, Stephen. (2001a). Cultures of Death: Suicide in Medieval Europe and Japan. *The Medieval History Journal* 4, 241-257.

_____. (2001b). *Milites,* Knights and Samurai: Military Terminology, Comparative History, and the Problem of Translation. In B. Bachrach and R. Abels (Eds.). *The Normans and their Adversaries at War.* (167-184). Suffolk, UK: Boydell and Brewer.

Mumford, Ethel Watts. (1906). The Japanese Book of the Ancient Sword. *Journal of the American Oriental Society* 26(2): 334-410.

Ñāñananda, Bhikkhu. (1997). *Concept and Reality in Early Buddhist Thought.* Kandy, Sri Lanka: Buddhist Publication Society.

Ñāṇamoli, Bhikkhu and Bhikkhu Bodhi (2001). *The Middle Length Discourse of the Buddha: A Translation of the* Majjhima Nikāya. Somerville, MA: Wisdom Publications.

Nishitani, Keiji. (1995). The Japanese Art of Arranged Flowers. J. Shore (Trans.). In R. C. Solomon and K. M. Higgins (Eds.), *World Philosophy: A Text with Readings.* New York, NY: McGraw Hill.

Nukariya, Kaiten. (1913). *The Religion of the Samurai: A Study of Zen Philosophy and Discipline in China and Japan.* London: Luzac & Co.

Osho. *Finger Pointing to the Moon: Discourses on the Adhyatma Upanishad*. London: Element Books, 1994.

Oyler, Elizabeth. (2005). *Swords, Oaths, and Prophetic Visions: Authoring Warrior Rule in Medieval Japan*. Honolulu, HI: The University Press of Hawaii.

Picone, Mary. (2012). Suicide and the Afterlife: Popular Religion and the Standardization of 'Culture' in Japan. *Culture, Medicine, and Psychiatry* 36: 391-408.

Picken, Stuart D.B. (2002). *Historical Dictionary of Shinto*. London: The Scarecrow Press, Inc.

Pinguet, Maurice. (1993). *Voluntary Death in Japan*. R. Morris (Trans.). Cambridge, UK: Polity Press.

Plato. (1997). *Phaedo*. G.M.A. Grube (Trans.). *Plato Complete Works*. John M. Cooper (Ed.). Indianapolis, IN: Hackett Publishing.

Random, Michel. (1978). *The Martial Arts*. London: Octopus Books Limited.

Ratti, Oscar, and Adele Westbrook. (1973). *The Secrets of the Samurai: A Survey of the Martial Arts of Japan*. Rutland, VT: Tuttle Publishing.

Ray, Reginald A. (2004). *In the Presence of Masters*. Boston, MA: Shambhala.

Reichhold, Jane. (2008). Introduction. In *Bashō: The Complete Haiku*. Tokyo: Kodansha International.

Reps, Paul and Nyogen Senzaki. (1998). *Zen Flesh Zen Bones: A Collection of Zen and Pre-Zen Writings*. Boston, MA: Tuttle Publishing.

Reuter, Christoph. (2002). *My Life is a Weapon: A Modern History of Suicide Bombing*. Princeton, NJ: Princeton University Press.

Bibliography

Richard, Timothy. (1907). *The Awakening of Faith in the Mahāyāna Doctrine.* Shanghai: Christian Literature Society.

Rinpoche, Kalu. (1986). *The Dharma: That Illuinates All Beings Like the Light of the Sun and the Moon.* Albany, NY: SUNY Press.

Rinpoche, Sogyal. (2009). *The Tibetan Book of Living and Dying.* San Francisco, CA: Harper.

Rinpoche, Tarthang T. (1975). *Mind in Buddhist Psychology.* H. V. Guenther and L.S. Kawamura (Trans.). Emeryville, CA: Dharma Press.

Saddhatissa, H. (1970). *Buddhist Ethics: Essence of Buddhism.* London: George All & Unwin Ltd.

Śāntideva. (1970). *Entering the Path of Enlightenment: The Bodhicaryāvatāra of the Buddhist poet Śāntideva.* M.L. Matics (Trans and Ed). London: Collier-Macmillan.

Sato, Hiroaki. (1995). *Legends of the Samurai.* Old Saybrook, CT: Konecky & Konecky.

Sato, Kanzan. (1983). *The Japanese Sword.* Tokyo, Japan: Kodansha International.

Scalambrino, Frank. (2015a). *Full Throttle Heart: Nietzsche, Beyond Either/Or.* New Philadelphia, OH: The Eleusinian Press.

_____. (2016a). *Introduction to Ethics: A Primer for the Western Tradition.* Dubuque, IA: Kendall Hunt Publishing.

_____. (2016b). *Meditations on Orpheus: Love, Death, and Transformation.* Pittsburgh, PA: Black Water Phoenix Press.

_____. (2011). *Non-Being & Memory: A critique of pure difference in Derrida and Deleuze.* (Doctoral Dissertation). Retrieved from ProQuest. (UMI: 3466382).

_____. (2014). Samsara and Nirvana. In D. Leeming, (Ed). *Encyclopedia of Psychology & Religion*, 2nd Edition, (pp. 1595-1602). New York: Springer. A substantial revision of: Scalambrino, F. (2009). Samsara and Nirvana. In D. Leeming, (Ed). *Encyclopedia of Psychology & Religion*, 1st Edition, (pp. 245-260). New York: Springer.

_____. (2016c). The Shadow of the Sickness Unto Death. In K. S. Decker, et al. (Eds.). *Breaking Bad and Philosophy*. (pp. 47-62). New York: Palgrave.

_____. (2015b). The Temporality of Damnation. In R. Arp and B. McCraw, (Eds.). *The Concept of Hell*. (pp. 66-82). New York: Palgrave.

Seward, Jack. (1969). *Hara-Kiri: Japanese Ritual Suicide*. Tokyo, Japan: Tuttle Publishing.

Shigesuke, Taira. (1999). *Code of the Samurai*. T. Cleary, (Trans.). Boston, MA: Tuttle Publishing.

Shulman, David. (1980). *Tamil Temple Myths: Sacrifice and Divine Marriage in the South Indian Saiva Tradition*. Princeton, NJ: Princeton University Press.

Shunzō, Sakamaki. (1967). Shinto: Japanese Ethnocentrism. In C.A. Moore (Ed.). *The Japanese Mind: Essentials of Japanese Philosophy and Culture*. (pp. 24-32). Honolulu, HI: The University Press of Hawaii.

de Silva, Lynn A. (1979). *The Problem of the Self in Buddhism and Christianity*. London: Macmillan Press.

Sōhō, Takuan. (1988). *The Unfettered Mind: Writings from a Zen Master to a Master Swordsman*. W.S. Wilson (Trans.). Tokyo, Japan: Kodansha International.

Sugawara, Makoto. (1988). *Lives of Master Swordsmen*. Tokyo, Japan: East Publications.

Suzuki, Daisetz Teitarō. (2006). *Zen Buddhism: Selected Writings of D.T. Suzuki*. London: Doubleday.

Suzuki, Shunryu. (2011). *Zen Mind, Beginner's Mind*. Boston, MA: Shambhala.

Bibliography

Takeuchi, Seiichi. (2015). *Flower Petals Fall, but the Flower Endures*. M. Brase (Trans.). Tokyo, Japan: Japan Publishing Industry Foundation for Culture.

Teshi, Furukawa. (1967). The Individual in Japanese Ethics. In C.A. Moore (Ed.). *The Japanese Mind: Essentials of Japanese Philosophy and Culture*. (pp. 228-244). Honolulu, HI: The University Press of Hawaii.

Thondup, Tulku. (1996). *Masters of Meditation and Miracles*. Boston, MA: Shambhala.

Tjardes, Tamara. (2003). *One Hundred Aspects of the Moon: Japanese Woodblock Prints by Yoshitoshi*. Santa Fe, NM: Museum of New Mexico.

Turnbull, Stephen R. (1977). *The Samurai: A Military History*. New York, NY: Macmillan Publishing Co.

Williams, Paul. (2008). *Mahāyāna Buddhism: The Doctrinal Foundations*. London: Routledge.

Woodward, F.L. (1922). The Ethics of Suicide in Greek, Latin and Buddhist Literature. *Buddhist Annual of Ceylon* Vol. 4 (Colombo, Ceylon: W.E. Bastian & Co.

Wright, Dale S. (2000). *Philosophical Meditations on Zen Buddhism*. Cambridge, MA: Cambridge University Press.

_____. (2009). *The Six Perfections: Buddhism and the Cultivation of Character*. Oxford: Oxford University Press.

Yamamoto, Tsunetomo. (2011). *Hagakure – The Way of the Samurai*. In The Samurai Series. J.H. Ford and S. Conners (Eds.). El Paso, TX: El Paso Norte Press.

Yixuan, Linji. (2008). *The Record of Linji*. R.F. Sasaki (Trans.). Honolulu, HI: University of Hawaii Press.

Young, Jerome. (2002). Morals, Suicide, and Psychiatry: A View from Japan. *Bioethics* 2: 412-424.

ABOUT THE AUTHOR

ဢ   ၓ

Professor Frank Scalambrino holds degrees in both psychology and philosophy, and graduated with his Ph.D. from Duquesne University in August of 2011. He is the first person in the history of Western philosophy to explicitly solve the problem of "non-being."
He has received recognition for teaching excellence in Ohio, Texas, Pennsylvania, and Illinois.
Before age 27 he founded a Community Mental Health Suicide Prevention Respite Unit and Clinical Intervention Center, and has worked in various direct service provision capacities in psychiatric emergency rooms and trauma settings, such as Mercy Medical Center (Canton, OH), the University of Pittsburgh Medical Center (UPMC Braddock), and the Tuscarawas County Health Department.
He was inducted into Chi Sigma Iota, the National Counseling Honor Society in 2003, and is a member of Beta Theta Pi (Kenyon College).
Professor Scalambrino has been teaching university-level courses since January, 2004, and he has taught graduate coursework
in both philosophy and psychology departments in Illinois and Texas.
He regularly teaches the history of philosophy, ethics, critical thinking, metaphysics, and the content of this book.
His recent publications include:
Full Throttle Heart (The Eleusinian Press, 2015), *Social Epistemology and Technology* (Rowman & Littlefield International, 2015), *Meditations on Orpheus* (Blackwater Phoenix, 2016), and *Introduction to Ethics: A Primer for the Western Tradition* (Kendall Hunt, 2016). His work has appeared in *The Review of Metaphysics*, *Philosophical Psychology*, *Phenomenology and Mind*, *Topos*, *Reason Papers*, *Philosophy in Review*, *Social Epistemology Review and Reply Collective*, and the *Internet Encyclopedia of Philosophy*.

Made in the USA
Lexington, KY
05 April 2017